Anguilla

Tranquil Isle of the Caribbean

Brenda Carty
history and constitution by
Colville Petty

CARIBBEAN

First published 1997 by
MACMILLAN EDUCATION LTD
London and Basingstoke
*Associated companies and representatives in Accra, Banjul,
Cairo, Dar es Salaam, Delhi, Freetown, Gaborone, Harare,
Hong Kong, Johannesburg, Kampala, Lagos, Lahore, Lusaka,
Mexico City, Nairobi, São Paulo, Tokyo*

ISBN 0-333-65966-X

10	9	8	7	6	5	4	3	2	1
05	04	03	02	01	00	99	98	97	96

Printed in Hong Kong

A catalogue record for this book is available from
the British Library.

Acknowledgments
The authors and the publishers would like to thank the following who
have kindly given permission for use of copyright material: Kathy Janzan
for the banana bread recipe from ABC of *Creative Caribbean Cookery*,
Macmillan Education Ltd; Telcine Turner for the poem 'Dancing Poinciana'
from *Song of the Surreys*, Macmillan Education Ltd; General Post Office,
Anguilla for stamps.

Every effort has been made to trace the copyright holders but, if any have
been inadvertently overlooked, the publishers will be pleased to make the
necessary arrangement at the first opportunity.

Front cover photograph by Michael Bourne.
Back cover painting reproduced by courtesy of Aileen Smith: *Millround.*

Government House
Anguilla

28 October 1995

It is with great pleasure that I write this foreword to the excellent guidebook, *Anguilla – Tranquil Isle of the Caribbean*, which Brenda Carty and Colville Petty have skilfully cooperated to produce. I do so since I can claim involvement in the exercise, having first discussed the idea with Macmillan Caribbean and persuaded the publishers to add Anguilla to their existing collection of titles.

The guidebook will be of interest to all tourist visitors to Anguilla. Equally it will appeal to residents of this beautiful island anxious to know more about the history and traditions of their island home.

The skills of the two co-authors are well matched. Mrs Carty contributes her experience in teaching and as a journalist reporting on day-to-day news from Anguilla, while Mr Petty makes full use of his knowledge as Anguilla's leading historian and a former senior public servant.

Readers will find here something to meet most of their needs. There are clearly written chapters on the history of the island and its people, information about local wildlife and even a glimpse into the fascinating world under the surrounding seas. The past is present, with references to the island's salt production industry and the origins of our very special boat racing traditions. Taking readers to Anguilla's territorial limits, special mention is made of Sombrero Island and the lighthouse there to protect international shipping. And then, of course, there is information about Anguilla's outstanding hotels, which have earned this island international repute for their acclaimed standards of hospitality.

I can commend the book to everyone interested in Anguilla.

Alan W Shave
Governor
1992–1995

Contents

North Ridge *opposite* (BRENDA CARTY)

(BRENDA CARTY)

(MICHAEL BOURNE)

| PART I |

Perspectives
on
Anguilla

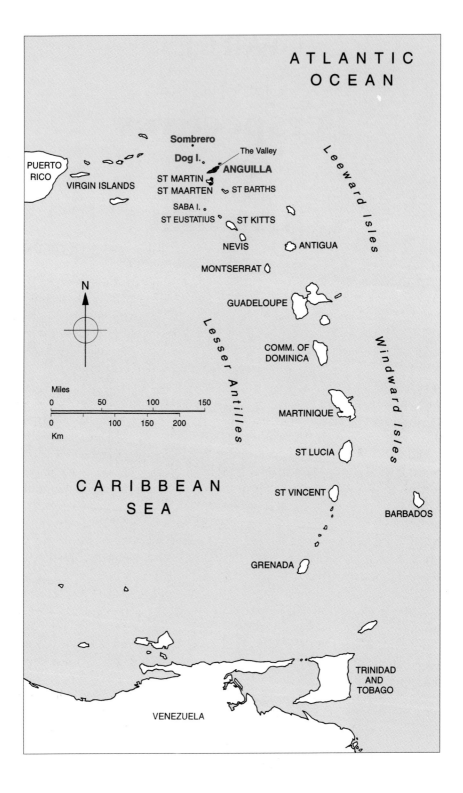

| 1 |

The land

Anguilla is the most northerly of the Leeward Islands, situated at 18°N and 63°W, lying between the Caribbean Sea and the Atlantic Ocean in a south-west, north-east direction. It is 146 miles (235 km) east of Puerto Rico, with St Martin six miles (10 km) to the south. Both islands serve Anguilla from their international airports.

Anguilla means 'eel' in Spanish and French, an apt description of this long, narrow island, although it is not known by which country it was given its name. A mere sixteen miles (26 km) long and three miles (5 km) broad at its widest point, with an area of just thirty-five square miles (90 sq km), Anguilla boasts some forty miles (64 km) of coastline. Its many beautiful, white sand beaches are among the best you can find in the Caribbean or even the world and these, together with crystal-clear blue sea, underwater reefs with a plethora of tropical sea creatures and a pleasant climate, have helped make Anguilla the chosen holiday destination of the discerning traveller.

Indeed, the climate is ideal, with tropical temperatures cooled by north-easterly trade winds throughout the year. The average temperature is 80°F (27°C), which drops a few degrees at night. Rainfall is low, with an average of thirty-five inches (88 cm) per year. There is no rainy season, although rain is usually expected in May and November. However, showers are sparse and a rainy morning can quickly turn into a beautiful tropical day. The setting sun provides many glorious photo-opportunities.

Anguilla is a very flat island, with only a few hills, the highest point being 215 feet (66 m) above sea level. It consists mainly of limestone, giving rise to some interesting caves (see Chapter 17, page 103 and Chapter 20, page 114), and coral, with small outcrops of volcanic rock. There are no rivers or streams on the island, but several ponds, some of which are salt-bearing.

Much of the natural vegetation is scrub, although Anguilla has some attractive tropical trees, shrubs and flowers which have flourished partly because of a reduction in the practice of cutting down trees for fuel and partly because until 1995 there had been no significant hurricane damage for over thirty years.

SERIOUS HURRICANES IN ANGUILLA

1822	Anguilla devastated by hurricane.
1898	Serious damage caused.
1922	Several houses damaged.
1950	*Hurricane Janet*: 411 houses destroyed or badly damaged.
1955	*Hurricane Alice*: 626 houses destroyed or damaged; extensive damage to shipping.
1960	*Hurricane Donna* devastated Anguilla.
1979	*Hurricane Frederick* caused loss of livestock and crops.
1984	*Hurricane Klaus* caused extensive damage to ships; Mv *Sarah* and the famous schooner, *Warspite*, were sunk.
1995	Hurricane Luis: severe damage to home, boats, vegetation and communications.

There are many small islands close to and belonging to Anguilla; Scrub Island in the north-east, Anguillita in the south-west, Prickly Pear and Dog Island to the north-west. Sombrero, about forty miles (64 km) to the north-west of Anguilla, is probably the best known because of its famous lighthouse and because of its economic significance to Anguilla during the last century (see Chapters 9 and 15, pages 51 and 81). The smallest and most accessible island off Anguilla is Sandy Island, a short boat ride from Road Bay (see Chapter 23, page 127).

| 2 |
The people

The people of Anguilla are known for their friendliness, their pride and their independent character. They are no strangers to hardship. Historically Anguillians have had to earn their living from farming arid, infertile soil, from fishing, from boat-building and from trading with neighbouring islands. As recently as fifty years ago all trade was conducted by schooner or sloop.

The ancestry of Anguillians is predominantly African, their forebears having arrived on the island as slaves to work on the sugar estates (see Chapter 10, page 59).

The present population of Anguilla is 9660, a 38 per cent increase from the previous census in 1984, when 6987 people were registered. This in turn represented a more than 50 per cent increase from 1819, when there were just 3080 residents.

(MICHAEL BOURNE)

Ebenezer Methodist Church   (ANDRIOLA/CARTY)

Religion has always been important to Anguillians and today most families are still deeply attached to their church life. The Anglican church was firmly established in Anguilla by the early eighteenth century and Anglicans today represent 36 per cent of the population. The Wesleyan Methodist Missionary Society was founded in Anguilla in 1813 by an Anguillian, John Hodge. The Road Methodist Chapel was built in 1828 and Ebenezer Methodist Church in The Valley followed two years later (see Chapter 16, page 91): Methodists account for 33 per cent of the present population. The Baptist and Catholic churches were established much later and today 7 per cent of the population is Baptist and 3 per cent Catholic, with a further 7 per cent being Seventh Day Adventists. Many of the churches in Anguilla are well worth a visit and are described in Part III.

The literacy rate is high in Anguilla, with 90 per cent of the population able to read and write. Education is based on the British system and all children receive free education until the age of seventeen. There are six primary schools in different districts of the island and one comprehensive school in The Valley, which all children attend from the age of eleven. There is a link-up in the library with the University of the West Indies Distance Learning Programme and students can complete at least one year of university studies from Anguilla.

| 3 |
Resources and livelihoods

Tourism

Prior to the development of tourism in the late 1970s and early eighties, Anguilla was an undeveloped island with very few opportunities for employment: indeed there are probably as many Anguillians living abroad today as there are in Anguilla itself, driven overseas by economic necessity. Many went to Aruba, Curaçao and Trinidad to work in the oil refineries; some went to work in the cane fields in St Kitts, the Dominican Republic and Cuba (see Chapter 11, p. 64). Others went to the USA or Britain and there are still many Anguillians living in Slough, England and New Jersey, USA. Traditionally therefore the economy of the island depended greatly on remittances from abroad to augment the income generated from local employment in fishing, trade between the islands and the salt industry, which was seasonal.

In 1980 the government began a programme to develop Anguilla as an upmarket tourist destination and in consequence the economic base of the island has shifted dramatically. In 1982 there were 17,000 visitors to the island; by 1992 this had increased to 93,000 and the number is growing. The number of people employed in Anguilla in 1974 was just over 1000 with unemployment at 40 per cent. In contrast, at the census in 1992 there was a workforce of over 4000, with an unemployment rate of just 7 per cent, and more than half of the workforce is currently employed directly or indirectly in tourism. Increasing employment prospects have led many expatriate Anguillians to return home.

The construction industry is one that has benefited directly from the development of tourism and the island now boasts several top-quality hotels, guest houses and villas, with a total of 1000 rooms, most of which are occupied during the height of the season from December to April. Small developments are still being built. Tourism-related industries have also burgeoned and include airline charters, car rentals, taxi and bus tours, art galleries, boutiques and water sports.

Boat-building

Anguillians are an island people, historically dependent upon the sea. As a result, boat-building became and remains a local craft: schooners as large as 150 tons used to be built at Sandy Ground, Forest Bay, Blowing Point and Island Harbour. Many Anguillians have made a name for themselves as boat builders, one of the most famous being Egbert Connor, who built the original *Bluebird*, a local racing boat. He was building racing boats until 1984, a few years before he died, and was still using the traditional tools of the past 200 years.

Indeed the method of building racing boats has not changed greatly over the years, the main difference being in the use of plywood for the frames and of epoxy adhesives to secure white pine planking on to the frames. Traditionally masts were made of wood, although today they are mostly aluminium, and dacron has replaced light canvas as the preferred material for sails. Today a boat can be built in just three weeks, especially when August week is approaching (see Chapter 6, page 25), and owners and crew are keen to participate.

Apart from racing boats the market today is for commercial fishing boats, sports fishing boats, leisure cruisers, ferry boats, high-speed

(ANDRIOLA/CARTY)

run-abouts and tender dinghies. There are several boat builders on the island, the largest being Rebel Marine, which has been building custom-made boats for Anguilla and the overseas market for many years.

A modern method of boat building for wooden boats is the WEST system (wood, epoxy, saturation technique) in which the epoxy coating serves as both adhesive and protective coating for the wood. The ferry boat service between St Martin and Anguilla uses boats of this type since they are lighter than their fibreglass counterparts. However, fibreglass boats are still produced on the island as they are faster to build and therefore less expensive to buy.

Other industry

Of the other traditional industries, fishing retains its importance to Anguillians even though the number employed is relatively small. Fishermen produce annually between 300 and 500 tonnes of fish, lobster and conch, most of which finds its way to restaurants on the island where fresh seafood is a speciality. There has been increased emphasis placed on other food production too. Two recent projects at the Agriculture Department in The Valley are rabbit rearing and bee keeping, the honey from Anguillian bees being of high quality. In 1982 the growing of lettuce by hydroponics was established and over 45,000 heads of lettuce are now produced monthly, supplying the needs of hotels, restaurants and stores in Anguilla, as well as being exported to St Martin/St Maarten, St Barths and St Thomas. Other agricultural enterprises on Anguilla include five chicken farms and around 150 part-time farmers who own a pig or two, keep several goats and do backyard gardening on about half an acre of land, thus ensuring that locally grown sweet peppers, tomatoes, cabbages and pumpkins are usually available.

Hand in hand with tourism has come the development of Anguilla's infrastructure. The European Union has funded several projects, including a road programme, completed in 1993, involving the paving of some five miles of road at a cost of US$4 million, and a water development programme to improve distribution of water throughout the island. British aid to Anguilla is substantial and over a four-year period amounted to US$16 million. Projects have included the building of a new hospital, library, post office, old people's home, prison and court house (see Chapter 16, page 89), and these in turn have led to growth in civil service employment, including education, police, health and customs.

IMPORT DUTY

Duty on imported goods provides 45 per cent of total government revenue in Anguilla, the main duty earners being vehicles, petrol, beer, wine, soft drinks, aluminium doors, tiles, plywood, T-shirts and wooden doors. Duty on wine and beer is 30 per cent, which visitors to the island will find reflected in restaurant prices.

Offshore finance

Anguilla is keen to attract investors and has been ideally placed to encourage an offshore finance industry due to its zero tax jurisdiction with no personal, corporate or withholding taxes and no restrictions on foreign exchange. It is a British Dependent Territory with the advantages of a sound legal framework, political and economic stability, and good telecommunications. Well regulated financial services and international professional expertise, combined with full confidentiality and banking secrecy, are making an increasingly important contribution to Anguilla's prosperity.

| 4 |
Heritage and culture

Houses

The building method most widely used throughout the Caribbean used to be **wattle and daub**, where a latticework of twigs and branches was simply covered with mud and allowed to dry in the sun, and the roof was usually made from thatched palms. Sadly, the one remaining local example was destroyed by Hurricane Luis.

However, other traditional styles of building can still be seen in Anguilla. Some older style homes are made of **shingles**, wooden tiles, although many of these are also fast disappearing and the Anguilla National Trust is currently trying to preserve them. Elaborate wooden latticework decoration is still in evidence, often on verandahs and around the eaves of houses. This '**gingerbread**' design is thought to have derived its name from the practice of German pastry makers, well-known for their ornately decorated gingerbread. Many of these buildings have been preserved and converted into restaurants, offices and shops. Some more modern houses reflect outside influences but retain wooden railings and shutters to maintain the traditional Caribbean appearance. A good example of vernacular architecture is the White House at Sandy Ground (see Chapter 17, page 100).

An unusual sight to the visitor are **old brick ovens** still to be seen in the yards of a few of the older houses. The base of the oven is built from limestone and coral, upon which is constructed the rounded oven, measuring around five feet deep, four feet wide and three feet high (approximately 1 m by 1.5 m by 2 m). Inside, the oven is lined with bricks to hold the heat; the roof and sides are sealed with a mixture of coral, lime and mortar. There is a small opening in the front where the wood, and later the bread, is loaded.

The oven is heated by burning any available wood, including wood scraps and dead wood from nearby trees, and it takes about forty-five minutes for the bricks to reach a high temperature. Wood ash and hot

overleaf (MICHAEL BOURNE)

coals are raked into a small side outlet called an ash pit and the oven is then ready to be used for baking. During baking hot ash and coals remain in the ash pit and serve to keep the temperature constant. If the oven is too hot the metal covering on the outside of the pit is removed and some of the ash is raked out in order to lower the temperature. A long handled wooden tool with a flat, broad head, called a peel, is used to load and unload the bread, which takes about one hour to bake.

The whole process may not be as easy as turning on your gas or electric stove, or visiting the local bakery, but the resulting bread is excellent. One oven, in North Hill, is still in daily use baking bread for villagers, and at Koal Keel Restaurant in The Valley a renovated oven is on display and in use (see Chapter 16, page 92).

Music

Anguillians, like most West Indians, enjoy music. It has always been a part of the tradition in Anguilla and several excellent bands have been formed which have gained international success. Bankie Banx is well known in Europe and the USA as well as in the Caribbean for his band 'Bankie Banx Roots and Herbs'. He plays a variety of music from folk guitar, through rhythm and blues, reggae and jazz, all in his own unique style.

'Dumpa', Michael Martin, is one of the best steel pan players in the island and can be heard regularly at various locations including Johnno's Beach Bar at Sandy Ground (see Chapter 17, page 98). He has worked hard and successfully in the schools to form steel bands which have progressed rapidly. The steel pan originated in Trinidad and Tobago and the bands there are still the best in the Caribbean, producing a great variety of music. It is a skilled art to make the pans from the oil drums; the ones used by the school band were made by a craftsman from Antigua.

Calypso has spread throughout the islands, again from Trinidad, and was originally a development of African and French folklore and songs. The calypso is now often used to highlight a social or political current event and is usually gossipy and witty. It is becoming a popular form of music in Anguilla at Carnival time.

The Mayoumba Folkloric Group has been in existence since 1972 and continues to please audiences in Anguilla and the rest of the Caribbean under the leadership of Julian Harrigan. This versatile

An old brick oven *opposite* (ANDRIOLA/CARTY)

group of singers, instrumentalists and actors performs a variety of music in their own West Indian style.

Most hotels have good entertainment provided by the excellent musicians on the island, playing steel pans, guitar and keyboard.

Arts and crafts

There are several local artists in Anguilla as well as resident artists from overseas who work in a variety of mediums and produce some attractive and charming work, for which there are four main outlets. The **Devonish Art Gallery** at George Hill has some high quality wood sculpture and pottery as well as paintings from different artists. Courtney Devonish is a wood and stone sculptor and potter who is known internationally; he was born in Barbados but now lives and

Cheddie's carving studio   (BRENDA CARTY)

16

works in Anguilla. **Cheddie's Carving Studio** on the West End Road has some exceptional carving, mostly from a clever use of driftwood found locally. Cheddie is a local sculptor who has been carving since the age of nine. In addition to his driftwood carvings he imports seasoned mahogany and walnut and produces lifelike carvings, many of which relate to the sea and include fish, lobsters, shells and small boats. The **Arts and Crafts Centre** has a variety of pottery, paintings, shell craft and other crafts from local artists, while the **New World Gallery** has some exceptional paintings by local and foreign artists in all mediums, as well as a collection of artefacts from around the world.

Food and drink

The influence of many cultures is observed in the food and drink throughout the Caribbean, and Anguilla is no exception. Tropical fruit and fruit drinks are expected everywhere, as of course is rum. Friendly barmen are always happy to mix exotic drinks with equally fantastic names but here rum punch is a must. This mixture of rum, lime and sugar is usually much stronger than it tastes, so be warned!

RUM PUNCH
Make your own for friends at home. Just remember these proportions:

One of sour   *(lime juice)*
Two of sweet   *(sugar melted in water)*
Three of strong   *(rum)*
Four of weak   *(water)*

Mix together, add to ice and top with grated nutmeg.

For a milder drink try sorrel, made from red sorrel flowers, sugar, ginger and cloves. It tastes good and is customary at Christmas.

Not surprisingly for an island people, fish is always high on the menu. The 'catch of the day' is likely to be snapper, grouper or mackerel, and is prepared in many ways. Creole sauce is a favourite, using lime, tomatoes, onions and sweet peppers. Lobster and crayfish are excellent choices for the diner (see Chapter 20, page 115), as is conch – try conch fritters or conch chowder as a starter, or conch stewed, fried or in a salad as a main meal.

Conch chowder   (KATHY JANZAN)

A traditional and nutritionally balanced dish is peas and rice, using local pigeon peas. Pigeon pea soup is also very good. Other 'musts' are pumpkin, either in soup or as fritters, and fried or roasted plantain, a member of the banana family. Local desserts include sweet potato pudding, or pone, coconut tart and sugar cake. These are usually obtainable in bakeries, which are well known for their high standard of bread and other delicacies.

| 5 |
Sport and recreation

Boat-racing is Anguilla's national sport and is even more important than cricket, usually considered the traditional West Indian sport. Almost everyone on the island has a keen interest in the races, which have become very competitive, and many people are actively involved in racing, boat-building and sailing.

In times of hardship Anguillians have looked to the sea for their livelihoods, either directly through fishing, or indirectly as a thoroughfare to neighbouring islands. In the early part of the twentieth century when schooners transported workers from Anguilla to the Dominican Republic to work as cane cutters, the return journey was always a race home. This journey could take anything from four to twenty days and was a constant beat to windward. Families still recall how they watched with great anticipation for the first schooner to round the point at Sandy Ground or to arrive at the Forest. Fishing boats would also often race back home from a day's work, even after a long trip as far as 'England Deep'. After setting or hauling their pots the fishermen would wait for each other so that they could race home and the fishing boats are in fact the forerunners in style of today's racing boats.

Racing gradually became more of a sport in its own right and the first boat intended primarily for racing was built by Mac Owen of North Hill in the late 1930s. It was called *Violet*, after his daughter, and was eighteen feet (5.5 m) in length. Other boats built with racing in mind soon followed, and the August boat races became established (see Chapter 6, page 25). For many years boats were used for both fishing and racing, but about twenty-five years ago when the fishing boats started using outboard motors and more sophisticated equipment, the racing boats became increasingly specialised.

The racing that has evolved in Anguilla is unique to the island, especially the way in which the boats are fitted and handled. The traditional boats have no decking; they are generally between twenty and twenty-eight feet (6–9 m) in length, seven to nine feet (2–3 m) in width and with a mast of up to forty feet (12 m). There is no external ballast on the hull; instead large smooth rocks, iron, lead or bags of

19

page 22

THE WARSPITE

(BRENDA CARTY)

One of the most famous of the old wooden schooners was the *Warspite*, which sailed the waters of the Caribbean for nearly seventy years. She was owned by Captain Arthur Romney Carty who bought her in 1916 as a forty ton sloop named the *Gazelle*. At that time he altered the bow section, added eleven feet to her overall length and renamed her *Warspite* after the famous Royal Navy battleship.

From the beginning she was a fast boat and at that time was used mainly to transport men to the Dominican Republic to work in the cane fields. In 1929 changes were again made; the boat was cut in two and fourteen feet added in the centre, making her seventy-five feet long.

For many years the *Warspite* continued to transport workers to Santo Domingo along with the *Ismay, Eagle, Betsy* and *Murielle*. Following the decline of the sugar trade the *Warspite* transported goods between the smaller islands of the Caribbean and was used particularly to transport salt to Trinidad. For some years she was the supply ship for the Sombrero lighthouse, taking supplies and men every two weeks to the island.

It was a sad day for many Anguillians when in November 1984 Hurricane Klaus destroyed this two-masted, black-hulled boat, the last of Anguilla's wooden schooners.

(BRENDA CARTY)

Racing under way (BRENDA CARTY)

sand are used. Minute changes in this ballast or trim can often make the difference between victory or defeat, so the amount of ballast and its use is a technique which is vital to the outcome of the race. Sometimes ballast has to be thrown overboard during a race and even one of the crew may receive this treatment, although there is always a motor boat nearby for rescue purposes. There are usually nine to eleven men in the crew of the larger Class A boats, and fewer in the smaller Class B and C boats.

The races in Anguilla usually have two points; the boats first run before the wind or westward away from the shore to a stake boat or marker some miles out. Then they beat to windward, back to shore, to a buoy a few yards from the beach, which is the finishing post and must be touched by one of the crew. This in itself often creates great excitement as the boat in the lead cannot always touch the marker first.

An interesting aspect for the spectator, which is unique to Anguilla, is the 'hard lee' ruling. If two boats are on a collision course one must shout 'hard lee' and both have to tack away from each other at the last minute. Refusing to take the 'hard lee' results in disqualification. This rule causes dangerous situations and creates some exciting sailing and many heated arguments and discussions afterwards. Races take place regularly during the year on public holidays and other special occasions (see Chapter 6, pages 24 and 25).

Without a doubt, boat-racing takes pride of place among the sporting events of Anguilla. Nevertheless, cricket is avidly followed and encouraged among young Anguillians and football, athletics and basketball are all keenly contested. There are tennis courts throughout the island and visitors will find that most hotels have courts which they can use.

No account of recreation in Anguilla is complete without mention of the game of dominoes. Every village has a meeting place where men gather to compete and the enthusiasm for the game is obvious even from a distance, the crashing of dominoes on the table being part of the tradition.

| 6 |
Special events

Cultural education festival

Of interest to visitors and Anguillians alike is the Cultural Education Festival, held annually in February. Many of the old traditions are revived such as 'jollification', a collective means of helping to prepare land for planting. The people of the village used to gather at a designated home to work the land. It became quite a festive occasion with the women preparing food and drinks whilst the men were active with hoes and shovels. A re-enactment of salt reaping also takes place and is a means of teaching the young how previous generations were employed (see Chapter 15, page 79). Visitors can enjoy the spectacle of 'moko jumbies' on stilts and old-time string bands and can watch demonstrations of local cuisine and craft work.

An old-time string band   (COLVILLE PETTY)

Queen's Birthday Parade   (BRENDA CARTY)

Anguilla day

If you are in Anguilla in May, don't miss the spectacle of Anguilla Day
on 30 May, when Anguillians celebrate the 1967 revolution (see Chapter
11, page 64) with an official parade at Webster Park before the
Governor, Chief Minister and other officials. The parade is led by the
Royal Anguilla Police Force and most of the uniformed organisations on
the island take part. A major attraction is the round-the-island boat race
which takes an average of six hours, depending on weather conditions,
and is great fun to follow from the shore or the sea (see Chapter 5,
page 19). There are several other sporting events on this day.

Queen's birthday

The Queen's official birthday is celebrated in June with a parade in
the Webster Park. His Excellency the Governor is in full uniform, with
plumed helmet, and he inspects the Royal Anguilla Police Force and
other organisations participating. In the evening the Governor usually
hosts a cocktail party at Government House to which many leading
citizens are invited and a toast is given to Her Majesty.

August boat races

The first week in August is dedicated to boat racing and each day there are races in different locations. Most start at Sandy Ground but finish at Island Harbour on the Tuesday and at Blowing Point on the Wednesday. One of the highlights of the week is the series of races on Thursday, which are traditionally held at Meads Bay, and many crowds of spectators line the beach (see Chapter 5, page 19).

Carnival

The first week in August is also carnival week and celebrations include the choosing of a carnival queen, a calypso king and queen, a parade of bands on the street and many other events. Each year the costumes improve and more people become involved in the event but it is very small compared to carnival in some of the other islands, especially Trinidad, where the custom originated.

(COLVILLE PETTY)

DANCING POINCIANA

Fire in the treetops,
Fire in the sky.
Blossoms red as sunset,
Dazzling to the eye.

Dance, Poinciana,
Sway, Poinciana,
On a sea of green.
Dance, Poinciana,
Sway, Poinciana,
Regal as a queen.

Fire in the treetops,
Fire in the sky.
Crimson petals and white,
Stained with scarlet dye.

Dance, Poinciana,
Sway, Poinciana,
On a sea of green.
Dance, Poinciana,
Sway, Poinciana,
Regal as a queen.

Telcine Turner

| 7 |

Trees and flowers

Anguilla has some attractive tropical trees and shrubs and, although the natural vegetation is not as prolific as on many of the islands, it is considerably more lush than it was just twenty years ago when there was little but scrub and low bush.

Trees

One of the most striking trees on Anguilla is the **poinciana** (or flamboyant) found in hotel and private gardens. These trees have wide spreading branches, grow to a height of fifty or sixty feet (15–18 m) and are sometimes as wide as they are high. The flowers are bright

(BRENDA CARTY)
opposite (SEDDON AND LENNOX)

red and the leaves a delicate green. You may come across two or three of the less common yellow-flowering flamboyants on the island, which have large, compound leaves, divided into many small, feathery leaflets. The brown pods are about a foot in length and are very conspicuous when the leaves fall off the trees in the drier months.

The **frangipani** grows wild, especially in the north and east of the island. The trees are small compared to the cultivated ones, rarely more than ten feet in height, but the flowers, which are white in this wild variety, have an exotic smell. There is a white sap, which is poisonous and also will stain clothes, so they need to be picked with care (see Chapter 9, page 50).

Majestic **mahogany** trees border Coronation Avenue in The Valley, having been planted in 1937 to commemorate the coronation of King George VI. At right angles to this road is Queen Elizabeth Avenue, opened by Her Majesty Queen Elizabeth II in 1994, and bordered with **ficus benjamina** trees planted by the Anguilla Beautification Club, a group which has endeavoured to make Anguilla more attractive by planting trees in the grounds of many public buildings including the hospital, library and schools.

Most visitors wish for more trees on the beaches. The **manchineel** tree grows along the coast (mostly at Katouche Bay), but it is one to be avoided. The small apple-like green fruit is very poisonous and the leaves produce a sap which can blister badly. It is quite a large tree but one should not be tempted to shelter underneath during a shower, as the drips from the leaves can also blister the skin (see Chapter 9, page 50). The Carib Indians are said to have used the poisonous fruit of the manchineel for the tips of their arrows.

Mangroves are seen mostly alongside the ponds but some are also along the shore or even directly in the sea, especially at Little Harbour, Blowing Point and Corito (see Chapters 16 and 18, pages 97 and 104). The mangrove is a salt-tolerant plant indigenous to the tropics. In Anguilla three types are seen: the red, black and white mangrove and also the **buttonwood**, which is similar but not a true mangrove. The Anguilla Beautification Club has been replanting mangroves in several of the ponds and shorelines because the trees have a number of environmental advantages. They not only enhance the look of a pond but also provide nesting for birds, and where they are planted in a pond that is open to the sea provide a habitat for marine life which is safe from predators (see Chapter 19, page 109). They can protect beaches and the land from wave erosion and reduce soil runoff from the land in heavy rain. Bees produce particularly good honey from the flowers of the mangrove tree.

28

Salt-tolerant mangroves (MICHAEL BOURNE)

Tamarind tree (BRENDA CARTY)

The **neem** tree has proliferated since it was introduced to the island in the 1950s. It is drought resistant and grows quickly, hence its popularity with gardeners. It is an attractive tree, densely crowned, that grows to about twenty-five feet (8 m). It has light green leaves divided into many leaflets and the cream-coloured flowers have a very pleasant scent.

An evergreen shrub which grows in abundance along many of the beaches by virtue of its resistance to salt spray is the **sea grape**. It is commonly seen inland too and many have grown up to twenty feet (6 m) in height and are more properly trees. The sea grape leaf is broad, almost as big as a saucer, and turns into various shades of red and yellow as it dries. The flowers are a yellowish-white but, unless there is rain at the right time, these will often dry up and not become fruit. Many still survive and the fruit which grows in large bunches can be eaten when purple and ripe.

One of the tallest trees to be seen on the island is the **tamarind** tree, brought to the Caribbean in the early seventeenth century. There are many picturesque trees growing up to seventy feet (21 m) in height and providing welcome shade. The leaves are of a feathery nature and are light green. The pale yellow flowers are not particularly striking but develop into pods which are about two to six inches (4–10 cm) long. Children love to knock down the pods, open them up and suck the seeds, which are surrounded by a sticky brown pulp. Sometimes this pulp is removed and mixed with sugar to make tamarind balls or it can be made into a refreshing drink. There is a wild, much smaller variety of tamarind with inedible pods.

The **white cedar** tree grows wild throughout the island along many of the roadsides and, at varying times in the year depending on rainfall, will have pretty pink or white flowers. The cedar tree grows to a height of fifteen feet (4.6 m) or more. It can withstand drought and like many of the local trees, seems to grow miraculously out of pure rock.

BREADFRUIT TREE

Breadfruit is an excellent vegetable that can be baked, boiled, roasted, fried or used in soup.
The tree has attractive dark green, glossy leaves, produces fruit three times a year, and can bear for up to seventy years.

It was brought to the West Indies by Captain Bligh.

Yucca   (BRENDA CARTY)

The **yucca** is quite outstanding with its large pointed leaves, either growing straight from the ground or on a woody trunk. There are several in the gardens at Wallblake House and the large white flowers consisting of dozens of individual bell-like waxy blossoms are really superb. This member of the century-plant family can grow as high as twenty or thirty feet (6–9 m).

Other trees to look out for are the **almond**, the tall **breadfruit** tree, the **calabash** with its distinctive, large globe-shaped fruit and the **cassia** with pretty pink or yellow flowers. The easily recognisable **coconut palm** and other palms grow on some of the beaches and the taller ones provide welcome shade. The **cordia** is native to the Caribbean and has bright red flowers and plum-like fruits. Also worth seeing are the **loblolly**, with its large, knobbled trunk, the tall **lignum vitae**, the impressive **Norfolk Island pines** and the **turpentine** with its shiny bark.

Flowering shrubs

Whilst you are driving around Anguilla, you will notice the striking colours of the bougainvillea, the hibiscus and the oleander, all of which flower throughout the year.

31

Bougainvillea (BRENDA CARTY)

The commonly-seen red hibiscus (BRENDA CARTY)

Beautiful but poisonous – the pretty oleander (BRENDA CARTY)

The **bougainvillea** grows profusely and in many colours from white, pale pink, orange and crimson to the most common, purple variety. They are vines, with thorns on the stems which enable them to grow on fences, walls and the sides of houses. They can also be trimmed and shaped into attractive shrubs.

The **hibiscus** survives in the form of hedges, despite being one of the favourite treats of goats which, together with sheep, roam the island searching for food. It is always in flower, and each day new flowers appear and replace the ones from the previous day. There are many hybrid species but in Anguilla it is the red hibiscus that is seen most frequently.

The **oleander** is plentiful in Anguilla because it is poisonous to the goats and sheep. (It is also poisonous to humans – see Chapter 9, page 50). It blooms continuously in various shades of pink and white. The leaves are slender and pointed and the clusters of flowers grow on the ends of the branches. The oleander can grow up to twenty feet (6 m) but most are kept pruned.

Fruit trees

Anguilla is not known for its fruit trees as the rainfall is not sufficient for growth on a large scale. However, most homes have **banana**, **citrus**, **pawpaw (papaya)** and **mango** trees. There is an area at Sandy Hill, known locally as the mango garden, where there are many mango trees which produce very small but sweet mangoes, twice a year (see Chapter 21, page 120).

There are several lesser known fruits, indigenous to Anguilla. They will be difficult for the visitor to identify without a detailed description but those who are interested can look for the **genip**, **pommeserette**, **sapodilla**, **soursop** and **sugar apple**.

BANANA BREAD

To serve 6:
12 oz self-raising flour
2 teaspoons baking powder
1/2 teaspoon salt
3 oz butter
4 oz brown sugar
1/2 teaspoon grated lemon rind
2 eggs, beaten
1 teaspoon vanilla essence
4 bananas, mashed
2 oz chopped walnuts

Sift together the flour, baking powder and salt. Blend together the butter, sugar and lemon rind until light and creamy. Beat together the eggs, vanilla essence and banana pulp and add gradually to the creamed sugar mixture. After each addition add some of the flour mixture, folding in gently. When all ingredients are blended together add the walnuts. Mix well and pour into a greased loaf tin (8" x 4" 20 cm x 10 cm) bake at 350°F (180°C) for 1 hour.

(KATHY JANZAN)

Cacti and succulents

Cacti survive everywhere, even in the rockiest of places, and thrive because they store supplies of water in order to withstand drought conditions later. For this reason some grow even on the inhospitable island of Sombrero, including the yellow-flowering cactus, *Opuntia antillana*. The **turk's head** cactus, or **pope's nose** as it is known locally, resembles a large round elongated ball with a fez-like cap on the top. It produces a bright pink edible fruit. The turk's head cactus is seen in abundance at Windward Point, (see Chapter 21, page 119). It is one of the *cereus* family of cacti.

The **cholla** has cylindrical tubular links and inedible fruit. Some of these grow to a height of ten feet and are found in shaded areas. It is in the family of *opuntia* cacti.

The **prickly pear** is of the same family and is easily recognisable by its pear-shape and its covering of hair and prickles. The pear shapes are linked together and seem to grow out of each other. The prickly pear fruit looks rather like a green plum and is edible: it is used by some adventurous chefs on the island to make a delicious sauce.

The well-known and useful aloe plant grows wild and is good for soothing sunburn, and there are a number of sisal plants distinguished by the tall flower from the centre of the plant. Succulents which thrive on sea spray and thus can grow on Sombrero include **sea purslane**, and *Portulaca oleracea*, a small succulent herb.

Turk's head cacti (ANDRIOLA/CARTY)

Cholla cacti (ANDRIOLA/CARTY)

FLOWERS FOR REMEMBRANCE

(SANDRA BELL, ROYAL BOTANIC GARDENS, KEW)

Every year on Remembrance Sunday the British Secretary of State for Foreign and Commonwealth Affairs lays a wreath at the Cenotaph in London on behalf of the United Kingdom Dependent Territories. Wreaths are made using flowers and foliage from the Dependent Territories which grow in the gardens at Kew in Richmond and include native species of heather from the Falkland Islands, moss from the British Antarctic Islands, beach morning glory from the British Islands of the Indian Ocean and mangrove from the islands on the edge of the Polynesian archipelago.

Other plant species come from the British Virgin Islands, Montserrat, the Turks and Caicos Islands, St Helena, Gibraltar, Hong Kong and the Cayman Islands, which provides *Cattleya bowringiana*, the showy chocolate box orchid.

The crowning glory comes from Anguilla and is *Pedilanthus tithymaloides*, a member of the **euphorbia** family.

| 8 |
Birds and wildlife

Sea birds

The **brown booby** is the most common coastal booby in the West Indies. It is quite distinctive with chocolate-brown plumage, white lower breast and large pale yellow bill. Popular nesting areas for these birds are on Prickly Pear, Sombrero, Middle Cay and East End Cay as well as some of the other offshore islands, where they can be seen in great numbers.

The **brown pelican** is a large sea bird with an incredibly long bill and neck and a distinctive throat pouch. It is mostly brown with the upper part of its head and neck being white. It is seen at many of the beaches, flying high and then making an impressive dive for a fish, usually with a successful catch. When not looking for a meal, pelicans can be seen perched on rocks or boats.

The **laughing gull**, so called because of its raucous call, is the only species of gull which is found on Anguilla. In fact it is the only gull that nests in the Caribbean although other species are seen in

Brown booby (COLVILLE PETTY)

38

Magnificent frigate birds   (COLVILLE PETTY)

some of the islands. The laughing gull is recognisable by its black head which in winter is a mottled grey. It is seen on all the beaches, feeding from the surface of the water or trying to catch scraps from the pelicans.

The **magnificent frigatebird** is mostly black and has a deeply forked tail; the female has a white breast. It has a wingspan of more than six feet (nearly 2 m) and soars high above the sea before swooping down to catch a fish on the surface. Unlike the brown pelican, it does not land on the water because of the difficulty of taking to flight again.

A rarer sea bird in Anguilla is the **red billed tropicbird**. The cliffs at Little Bay provide a nesting area and habitat and this is the place you are most likely to see them (see Chapter 16, page 97). However, they are also seen nesting on other cliffs and the offshore cays. They plunge into the sea rather like the boobies and feed on squid and fish.

There are always several species of **sandpipers** on the beaches and around the ponds, and the **least tern** and the **royal tern** can be seen in Anguilla all the year round. **Noddy, sooty, least, bridled, roseate** and **royal terns** are found in relatively large numbers on Sombrero. Interestingly, birds' eggs formed a principal part of the diet of the labourers in the phosphate mines during the nineteenth century (see Chapter 15, page 81).

Great or common egret   (COLVILLE PETTY)

Pond birds

Common in all the ponds is the **black-necked stilt**, which is a very graceful wading bird identified by its contrasting black and white colouring and very long legs.

Two species of **egret** are most common in Anguilla. The **snowy egret** is generally all white and has long plumes hanging from its head, back and breast during the breeding season. It is a permanent resident on the island and can be seen wading quietly in the ponds. The smaller **cattle egret** is more commonly seen around the cattle or on newly-mown land, looking for insects. There are many that roost in the trees on the east side of the Road Salt Pond (see Chapter 17, page 98). The **great** or **common egret** is an uncommon though regular visitor.

The **great blue heron** is sometimes seen near the ponds. It is the largest of the herons and is between forty-two and fifty-two inches (106–132 cm) tall with a wing span of seven feet (2 m). It usually stands motionless in shallow water waiting for its prey. Despite its name, it is mostly grey in colour with a white head and long black plumes extending back from the crown. The blue heron comes to Anguilla in autumn and winter and can often be seen on the edge of the ponds and on the beaches and sea rocks.

The **lesser yellowlegs** is one of the most common shorebirds in the Eastern Caribbean but in Anguilla it is most often seen in the salt ponds and is known locally as the pond dipper. It has a long slender black bill and in flight its distinctive long orange-yellow legs project beyond the tip of its tail. Its upper parts are brownish-grey and its underside is white.

The only permanently resident duck is the **white-cheeked pintail**, seen in large numbers on all the ponds, usually in pairs. This small, grey-brown duck has prominent white cheeks and throat and a red base to its bill. The **blue-winged teal** is seen in large numbers during the winter months.

The **yellow-crowned night heron** is most frequently seen near the Road Salt Pond (see Chapter 17, page 98) or other salt ponds, but it is also found further inland. It is distinguished by its large head and heavy bill and by the white and black stripes near the eyes. Otherwise it is grey with black streaks on the back and wings. As its name suggests it is very active by night and is often heard around homes, even on the roofs.

Garden birds

Probably the most fascinating of the garden birds is the small and friendly **bananaquit**, often called yellow bird. It is always ready for food, especially a little brown sugar or sugar water, and will come into homes and hotels searching for some. The bananaquit is black above with a bright yellow breast and underparts. It feeds on nectar, fruit and small insects.

Of the **doves**, the **turtle** or **zenaida dove** is Anguilla's national bird and is seen searching for food on the ground. It is mostly brown with a pretty pink mottled breast and a long pointed tail with black and white tips. It has a low, soft cooing call. The **common ground dove** is smaller and seen mostly on the ground as the name implies, with head bent down looking for food. It is mainly brown and not as attractive as the turtle dove.

The cheeky bananaquit   (R P FFRENCH)

Hummingbird   (COLVILLE PETTY)

A common inland bird is the popular **hummingbird**. In Anguilla there are two species; the **green throated carib** and the **Antillean crested**. They are fascinating birds especially as they hover for so long and work hard gathering nectar.

Another small bird, often to be seen with the bananaquits, is the **Lesser Antilles bullfinch**. The female is brown and the male is black with a red throat.

A much larger bird which, like the bananaquit, can be quite tame when fed, is the **pearly-eyed thrasher** which resembles a large thrush and has piercing eyes. It is known locally as pawpaw bird because of its love for that fruit in particular. It has two voices, one very melodious and the other a quite raucous call of alarm or annoyance.

Quietly waiting on the telephone wires or the tops of trees is the **sparrow hawk** or **American kestrel**, known locally as a killy killy. It has a brownish-black back and tail, with spotted underparts and two distinctive black stripes on the side of its face. It will make a sudden swoop to catch an unsuspecting lizard or baby chick for its meal.

The **chinchary** or grey king bird, the **grassquit** and the **yellow warbler** are amongst the other birds frequently seen on the island.

Other wildlife

There is very little wildlife in Anguilla apart from the birds. Most common are the many **ground lizards**. These vary in size from four inches (100 cm) to six inches (150 cm), without measuring the tail, and usually appear between 9 am and 3 pm. During the shorter days of January to March you are unlikely to see them at all: they stay in their holes to conserve warmth. There are three species on Sombrero, the slate-black **amieva corvina**, which is the most common, the **gecko** and the **anolis**. Ground lizards eat all kinds of insects, snails, maggots and wood roaches, and also berries and fruits, the flowers of succulent plants and birds' eggs.

Iguanas have been sighted in the past few years but these have declined in numbers during the last fifty years as their habitat has been destroyed. At the last investigation it was estimated that only forty to fifty remain, many of which are in the area between Little Bay and Shoal Bay (see Chapter 20, page 114).

There are **centipedes** and **scorpions** on Anguilla, but you are unlikely to see any unless you are walking in thick bush. There are no poisonous **snakes** on Anguilla.

(ANDRIOLA/CARTY)

Although not strictly wildlife, the many **goats** and **sheep** which roam the island deserve a mention here. It is traditional in Anguilla to keep a few animals and although they are no longer essential for food some people make a livelihood by selling them. These animals are a source of much concern to many visitors when they see how little food is available, especially during dry weather. They are a source of even greater concern to gardeners and landscapers who lose many of their plants to the goats. Some animal owners do manage to feed their stock and keep them under control but it is difficult in the dry season when there is so little grass.

| 9 |
The sea

Scuba diving

The Dive Shop at Sandy Ground (see Chapter 17, page 98) is Anguilla's only full-service Scuba Diving Centre, owned and operated by two instructors with Professional Association of Diving Instructors (PADI) qualifications. The Centre is open seven days a week and offers a range of courses from a beginner's one-day course to a five-day complete certification leading to an internationally recognised Open Water Certificate for diving. A comfortable power catamaran and all necessary equipment for the courses is available and equipment is also available for individual hire.

Sites

Anguilla is surrounded by reefs and small islands and there are plenty of good diving sites within easy reach. In 1990 several wrecks were sunk as part of a clean-up of Road Bay, where they had been wrecked in previous storms. These now provide some interesting dive sites and among those favoured by The Dive Shop are the MV *Ooesterdiep* at a depth of seventy-five feet (23 m) and the MV *Sarah* at eighty feet (24 m), together with the MV *Commerce*, sunk four years earlier. Each is home to large numbers of schooling fish. Further out in the bay, Sandy Island offers diving to a depth of seventy feet (21 m), with an abundance of **soft corals** and **sea fans** as well as **reef fish**. Other popular sites include Author's Deep, a dive of 110 feet (33 m), where there is abundant **black coral** and sometimes large fish, and Grouper Bowl, home of some of Anguilla's beautiful **hard coral** formations. Little Bay, with a depth of fifteen to thirty feet (4–9 m) is a calm sheltered site ideal for night dives and is a nursery area for small fish and marine life with good photographic potential.

In the east of the island Junk's Hole Bay is of particular interest (see Chapter 21, page 120). The wrecks of two Spanish merchant ships are to be found here, having run aground on 9 July 1772 soon after

midnight. The ships were the *Buen Consejo* and the *Jesus Maria y Jose*, on their way from Spain to Mexico and the Philippines as part of a fleet of sixteen ships. On board were fifty Franciscan friars with their personal possessions, which included many valuable religious items, and also cargo of iron, spices, textiles, books and money to pay taxes in Mexico. Everybody survived but the ships were lost and a number of valuable artefacts have been recovered. Investigation is continuing at the time of publication and for this reason the area has been declared a marine park (see page 51).

Snorkelling

Anguilla is a wonderful place to snorkel, with many shallow areas and reefs with an abundance of marine life. Equipment is available at many hotels on the island, and can also be rented at Shoal Bay (see Chapter 20, page 114). Amongst the best areas to snorkel are Sandy Island, Shoal Bay, Sandy Hill Bay, Little Bay, Shoal Bay West, Corito, Barnes Bay and Crocus Bay, where a wide variety of fish, starfish, shells, coral and sea plants can be seen. Especially conspicuous among the fish are the **angel fish**, **butterfly fish**, the brightly coloured **parrot fish**, and **red hind**, **grunt** and **queen triggerfish**, known locally as old wife.

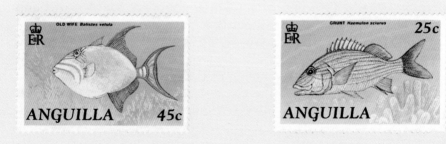

Coral reefs are among the most complex animal and plant communities in the world and are important for many reasons. Coral provides nutrients, shelter and breeding areas for many marine species and the reefs protect Anguilla's white sand beaches from erosion during storms and hurricanes. However, coral is fragile and may be damaged if it is touched or stood on, so snorkellers are asked to exercise care (see page 50). The most common species you will encounter are the **staghorn coral**, so named because it looks like deer antlers, and **brain coral**, which resembles the human brain.

There are very few dangers for the snorkeller in Anguillian waters. However beware of **sea urchins**, which can cause painful injury, and the **Portuguese man of war**, which is only rarely seen: most other jellyfish in Anguilla are harmless (see page 50). **Sharks** are seldom seen near to the shore and **barracuda**, although rather fierce-looking, are not known to attack. There are a number of **moray eels**, but again they will not usually attack. It is always advisable to snorkel with a companion and not to venture far unless you are very experienced.

Other marine life to look out for are large starfish and conch. **Starfish** are usually seen at a depth of six feet (2 m) or more crawling along the sea bed eating shells, urchins and small marine creatures. They range in colour from deep red to beige and some have attractive

The distinctive conch shell (MICHAEL BOURNE)

white markings. They are especially common at Sandy Ground and Rendezvous Bay (see Chapters 17 and 18, pages 98 and 104).

There are five species of **conch** in Anguilla; the **queen conch**, the **milk conch**, the **rooster-tail conch**, the **fighting conch** and the **hawkwing conch**. The queen conch is the most common and is the one used for food. It is also used to make jewellery and lamps or just as a decoration in homes and gardens. A tradition which is still heard today is the use of the conch as a horn to call people, especially to buy fish after a particularly large catch. The queen conch is very attractive with its pink flared lip and brilliant shades of pink inside. It is found from six to one hundred feet (2–30 m) deep on sea-grass beds, around coral reefs, on sand or on coral rubble. It eats by scraping algae from seaweed or sand with its rough-toothed 'tongue'. Unfortunately conchs are diminishing because of their popularity. Humans are the chief predators, but there are others such as the **spiny lobster** (which can eat away at the shell and reach the soft inside), **octopus**, **grouper**, **shark** and **sting ray**. Only conchs larger than seven inches (17 cm) in length can be caught and used for food and the hooker system is not allowed in Anguilla.

Other shells seen on the bottom of the sea are the **helmet**, which is fairly rare, **tritons** and **tulips**.

Fishing

The visitor who is keen to fish can always find a local fisherman who will be pleased to arrange a trip, or hotels can provide local contacts. Game fish are mostly **kingfish, tuna, mackerel, barracuda** and **dolphin**, a scaly fish known as dorado in other parts of the world. Spear fishing is prohibited except to residents of Anguilla. The majority of local fishermen catch fish in pots or traps, marked with a buoy at the surface, which are pulled every two or three days. Some of the pots are placed in fairly shallow water on or near the reef and **grunts, hinds, triggerfish**, the smaller **snapper** and other reef fish are caught. Other methods of fishing are trolling with a rod and line, hand lining, seine fishing and rig fishing. **Yellow-tailed snapper, jacks, cavalli, wahu** and **marlin** are usually caught on the line.

Some **lobsters** can still be seen on the reef but they are mostly caught far from shore and with very few exceptions are caught in traps or deep water pots, which are also used to catch **red snapper** and **grouper** (see Chapter 20, page 115). In order to protect lobster for future generations any caught must have a carapace longer than 3.74 inches (95 mm) and any crayfish or lobster bearing eggs must be immediately returned to its natural habitat.

Other marine life

Between February and May you may be lucky enough to see **whales**, especially in the channel between Anguilla and St Martin. This is the time of the annual migration of the humpback whales from the Arctic feeding grounds to the warmer waters of the Caribbean where they breed and calve.

There are four species of **turtle** in Anguillian waters; the **green turtle**, the **hawksbill**, the **leatherback** and the **loggerhead**. The first two are the most likely to be seen but unfortunately, as in many other areas of the world, their numbers are declining. The green turtle grows to between 200 and 500 pounds (90–200 kg) and does not breed until it is over twenty years old. It likes warm water shallow enough to allow the growth of sea-grass, its main food. The hawksbill is smaller, being from 80–140 pounds (35–60 kg) in weight and up to three feet (1 m) in length. It nests quite high up on the beach, even in the vegetation. Quite a number of turtles still nest on the quiet beaches in Anguilla and on the offshore cays. There is presently a five-year moratorium on the catching of turtles in Anguillian waters which it is hoped will help to preserve them.

A FEW WORDS OF WARNING

There are many beautiful and interesting sights in Anguilla, some of which you may not have encountered before. These few words of warning will help ensure your visit passes without incident.

Coral reef: The reef is ecologically important and very fragile. Visitors, and especially snorkellers, are requested to treat it with respect.

Fire coral: Avoid all red coral: most of it is fire coral, which gives a nasty sting.

Frangipani: The white sap is poisonous and will stain clothes.

Oleander: All parts of the plant are poisonous to animals and humans and the wood should not be used even for fires.

Manchineel: The fruit is poisonous and the sap can cause bad blisters. Do not shelter under manchineel trees, which are found mainly but not exclusively at Katouche Bay.

Mosquitoes: It is wise to be protected as mosquitoes can be plentiful after rain. However, there are no malaria-transmitting mosquitoes in Anguilla.

Portuguese man of war: These poisonous jellyfish are rarely seen in Anguillian waters. They are recognisable by the large purple balloon-like float on the surface and long tentacles below.

Sandflies: You will encounter sandflies on the beach after dusk, but they are not usually troublesome because of the constant breeze.

Sea urchins: Whilst not poisonous, the spines of a sea urchin can cause painful injury and are difficult to remove. Take care not to step or lean on one.

Snakes: Snakes are harmless and can be safely ignored.

N.B. It is illegal to remove any form of coral, sponges, starfish or shells, except dead ones found on the beach.

Marine parks

Certain areas have been designated as marine parks and are protected in order to preserve the natural heritage, nursery areas for fish, sea-grass, fragile reef and coral.

The marine parks are situated at Sandy Island, Dog Island, Prickly Pear, Shoal Bay East, Junk's Hole and Little Bay. Permanent moorings are established in these areas and anchoring is prohibited except at such moorings, which are for vessels under fifty-five feet (17 m) in length. A marine park mooring permit is needed for use of these buoys and can be obtained from the Fisheries Officer at the marine base at Sandy Ground (see Chapter 17, page 100 and Chapter 24, page 135).

The red buoys are for dive-boat use only and the white buoys are for other vessels. By law vessels must meet Anguillian customs and immigration requirements and have a cruising permit from their port of entry before applying for a marine park mooring permit. The moorings are for day time use only, until 7 pm. The purpose of the marine parks is to preserve the environment. Therefore visitors are requested to swim, snorkel and enjoy the beauty without interfering with the marine life.

The Sombrero lighthouse

Anyone sailing to Anguilla in their own yacht via the Anegada Passage will be familiar with the sight of the lighthouse on Sombrero. This tiny island, just three quarters of a mile long and a quarter of a mile wide, owes its significance to its strategic position in a major sea lane to the Caribbean and the Americas, highlighting the need for a lighthouse to ensure the safety of ships.

Shipping in the area increased significantly in the late 1830s and in 1842 the Royal Mail Packet Company began operating a steamship service between Britain and her trading partners. Their request for a lighthouse to the British Admiralty was given low priority until one of the company's ships ran aground on Horseshoe Reef near Anegada in the British Virgin Islands in 1859. Another ship was lost off Tortola in 1867, by which time plans for the construction of a lighthouse were on the drawing board but kept on hold pending ownership disputes between Britain and the United States.

The lighthouse finally came into service on the night of 1 January 1868. It was a wrought-iron open framework structure supported and

A snorkeller's paradise *opposite* (BRENDA CARTY)

51

Sombrero's barren landscape   (COLVILLE PETTY)

strengthened by a large central column through which a narrow spiral stairway led to the lantern-room some 156 feet (48 m) above sea-level. The lamp (an Argand lamp with reflectors) had to be trimmed occasionally while its winding mechanism, which caused the reflectors to turn, was wound every two hours. The day-to-day operations of the lighthouse were in the hands of two keepers who were supervised by the Superintendent of the Phosphate Company (see Chapter 15, page 81). The lighthouse's lighting mechanism was upgraded in 1931 with a 'vapour incandescent mantle lighting system' which produced a flash of 200,000 candlepower every five seconds.

By the late 1950s the metal structure of the lighthouse had deteriorated considerably and it was decided to build a new lighthouse farther inland. Construction work began in early 1960 but when the building had reached about twenty feet (6 m) above ground Sombrero was struck by *Hurricane Donna* (see Chapter 1, page 4), causing considerable damage to the new structure, whilst the original lighthouse remained intact. The new lighthouse came into operation on 20 July 1962 (and the old lighthouse was demolished one week later). Its kerosene pressure light stands some 166 feet (51 m) above sea-level. The lighthouse is in use today with five staff, a Principal Keeper, three keepers and a cook, each of whom spends, in turn, six weeks on Sombrero followed by two weeks' leave in Anguilla.

After more than 125 years the Sombrero lighthouse continues to send its beams across the waves *opposite*   (COLVILLE PETTY)

| PART II |

From past to present

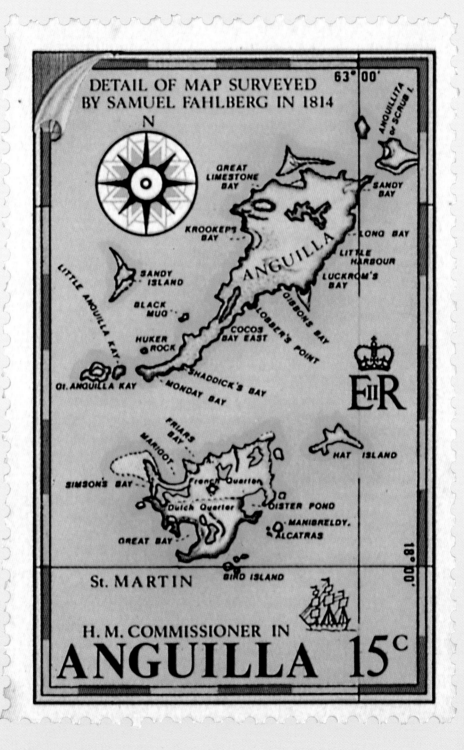

56

| 10 |
The early years

Settlement

The earliest known inhabitants of Anguilla were the Arawaks, an Amerindian people, who called it Malliouhana. They lived on the island from around 2000 BC until the arrival of the Europeans in the Caribbean towards the end of the fifteenth century. The first European to make contact with the Arawaks was Christopher Columbus, who described the women as 'very well built, with very handsome bodies and faces'.

The Arawaks were originally from the Orinoco region of South America and slowly made their way up through the chain of Caribbean islands by dug-out canoes. They were subsistence farmers who planted crops such as cassava, maize, sweet potatoes, tobacco, fruits and vegetables. They were also very good fishermen with a fondness for turtles and conchs.

Whilst there is no evidence that when the English colonised Anguilla in 1650 they met any of the Arawaks, the discovery of Amerindian artifacts at places such as Sandy Hill, the Big Spring at Island Harbour, Rendezvous Bay, Road Bay and Shoal Bay (see

---

ARAWAK CREATION

The Watcher in the Heights looked down
Upon the bare earth with a frown.
He caused the great Kumaka tree to grow until it touched the sky
And picking twigs and leaves He threw them down from high.

Those that fluttered turned to birds, even the little wren,
And others touching earth below became the animals and men.
Fish and other creatures swam in the waters wild
And sitting in the Heights above, the Watcher smiled.

Stephane Correia

Chapters 18 and 20, pages 104 and 114) illustrates their residence here and the richness of their culture. The English established their settlement probably at Road Bay or in the area around Cauls Pond. De Rochfort wrote:

At the part where it is widest, there is a lake around which a few English families settled for seven or eight years and where they cultivated tobacco, which is very much prized by those who value that article of commerce.

The colonists had hardly settled down when, in 1656, the Caribs, a warrior people from South America, raided the island and wiped out the settlement, killing almost all of the men, plundering and burning the houses and keeping the women and children for slaves. Further difficulties were experienced in 1666 when a French expedition consisting of 300 men attacked the island. Unable to defend themselves, the colonists set fire to their houses and fled to the woods. In 1688 others were forced to seek refuge in Antigua, where they were taken in three sloops following a joint Irish and French attack on Anguilla.

Despite these setbacks the colonists returned and continued to exploit the land but the poor returns from cotton, which had replaced tobacco as the island's cash crop, created considerable hardships and by the early eighteenth century they had turned to the production of sugar. Crucial to the success of sugar was a good supply of cheap labour, and in common with the other West Indian colonies, Anguilla's supply came from Africa. Sugar transformed a mainly white society of small farmers into a society of predominantly African slaves labouring on sugar estates.

Attacks by the French

The development of Anguilla's economy was frequently disrupted by European political conflicts which spilled over into the Caribbean. In 1744 three hundred Anguillians, assisted by two privateers from St Christopher (St Kitts), captured the French half of St Martin. The French retaliated on 21 May 1745 when two frigates and some small craft entered Crocus Bay where De la Touche with seven hundred men came ashore and attempted to take the island (see Chapter 17, page 102). It took Governor Hodge and a militia of 150 men about fifteen minutes to force them to retreat with thirty-two men killed and twenty-five (including De la Touche) wounded. Some fifty men were taken prisoner.

After this attack the Anguillians enjoyed relative peace which ended when the Revolutionary Government in France declared war on England in 1793. At first the battles were confined to Europe but, as with the earlier wars, the Caribbean eventually became embroiled in the conflict and Anguilla was invaded by the French in November 1796 when they landed four hundred men from two warships, *Le Desius* and *La Vaillante*, at Rendezvous Bay. The men advanced eastwards and destroyed the main settlements at South Hill and at The Valley where they 'burnt the little town, pulled down the church, stabbed men in their houses and stripped women of their clothes'. They also destroyed the island's trading vessels.

The Anguilla militia put up a brave fight but steadily lost ground to a strong and disciplined French force. They were eventually pushed eastward towards the Sandy Hill Fort where they halted the advance of the French. It has been claimed that when the Anguillians' ammunition ran out the fishermen cut off the lead balls from their sprat seines to load the cannons.

While the battle raged a fast sailing vessel was sent to St Kitts to summon assistance and a British frigate, the *Lapwing*, under the command of Captain Barton, was sent. On seeing the frigate sail down the channel between St Martin and Anguilla the French hurriedly abandoned their siege of the Sandy Hill Fort and took to their ships. The ensuing naval battle resulted in the loss of the two French ships while the *Lapwing* suffered only one dead and six wounded.

The war had a detrimental affect on the lives of the Anguillian people, who were already experiencing difficulties with sugar, which continued to be the main cash crop. Sugar production in Anguilla was never profitable, unsuited as it was to the island's shallow soil and low rainfall. Furthermore, the industry lacked capital and it was impossible for the white planters to operate big estates and hold large numbers of slaves. Diversification was their salvation and, in addition to sugar and rum, Anguillians exported cotton, indigo, fustic and mahogany.

Union with St Kitts

Conditions in Anguilla were influenced not only by European conflicts and the health of the economy but also by political expediency. The Leeward Islands Administration, of which Anguilla was part, was disbanded in 1816 and the various islands were then grouped into two political and administrative units, one of which comprised Anguilla, St Kitts, Nevis and the Virgin Islands. The British Secretary of State advised Governor Maxwell in St Kitts, by letter dated 6 May 1824, to 'take an early opportunity of recommending to the Legislature of St Christopher's [St Kitts] to pass an Act for augmenting the membership of the House of Assembly by the addition of a Representative of the Island of Anguilla'.

This suggestion was considered by the Government in St Kitts and a commission of inquiry was appointed to study the entire Anguilla situation. The commission recommended that Anguilla should be allowed to send a representative to the House of Assembly and this was accepted by the Government in St Kitts: Act No. 21 of 1825.

Although some thirty-five freeholders in Anguilla had signed a resolution in support of the legislative union with St Kitts, they quickly protested its implementation when they realised that their own council was to be dissolved. Their petition of 10 March 1825 to the Governor made the point that the legislative union placed Anguilla at a serious disadvantage because by sending only one representative 'we shall be imperfectly represented there'. Despite strong protests the union was forced upon the island's 3000 inhabitants. The Anguilla Council was replaced by a system of local government called the

Vestry in 1827 and the island was divided into three divisions, Road, Valley and Spring, for the purpose of elections.

The emancipation era

Social and economic conditions in Anguilla worsened during the 1830s when prolonged droughts destroyed all food crops and resulted in famine. Slaves made idle by the drought were allowed by their masters to go abroad and earn money, some of which they used to buy their freedom and that of their relatives. The money they sent back provided many benefits and so began a remittance-type economy upon which the Anguillian people subsequently depended for many years.

Slavery in Anguilla came to an end in 1838 when the St Kitts Legislature abolished the apprenticeship system provided for by the Emancipation Act of 1833. By this time the fragile sugar industry had virtually disappeared and most of the white planters had sold their land to the ex-slaves and returned to England. Some migrated to the USA. Those ex-slaves who lacked money with which to purchase land occupied estate lands which the whites had abandoned, while others occupied Crown land. Some rented lots for which they paid mainly in kind because of the shortage of cash. The ex-slaves grew food crops to meet household needs and Anguilla developed into a society of independent peasants who settled all over the island in order to utilise every available pocket of fertile land.

Emigration plan

Drought conditions persisted and during the 1840s the island experienced another period of economic depression. When the Lieutenant Governor of St Kitts and Anguilla informed the Secretary of State, Lord

Russell, about 'the distressed condition of the peasantry of Anguilla', Lord Russell instructed the Governor-in-Chief in Antigua to take all necessary steps to move the entire population of Anguilla to Demerara in British Guiana (now Guyana) which, like the larger Caribbean territories, was now experiencing a shortage of labour. The authorities in British Guiana wasted little time in following up the proposal and dispatched three vessels to Anguilla, where only a handful of Anguillians took up the offer. Other islands also opened their doors to the Anguillians, including Dominica, Antigua and Trinidad. The authorities in Trinidad offered them free passage and 'sufficient guarantee ... for the aged and infirm', but to no avail. In spite of the many hardships the Anguillian people had no intention of leaving the island en masse or permanently. Having become accustomed to supporting themselves they were not prepared to give up their independence and work for wages on sugar estates. One British official, who had described Anguilla as an 'assemblage of paupers', admitted that the people's love for their homeland did not permit them to emigrate. They preferred to starve rather than abandon the island. It was from a position of hopelessness, and against all official advice, that the Anguillians decided to stay at home and eke out a living. Their resolve ensured Anguilla's survival as a separate and distinct society.

Disfranchisement

The hardships which the Anguillians experienced during the latter part of the nineteenth century heightened their resentment of the forced union with St Kitts, which was strengthened constitutionally with the re-creation of the Leeward Islands Federation in 1871. They made their resentment known to Queen Victoria, whom they petitioned on 23 August 1872 to dissolve the union and administer Anguilla directly from Britain. One of their principal complaints was what they described as 'a most galling and oppressive system of direct taxation'. The Anguillians opposed the paying of tax on dogs, old houses and on land which produced nothing for most of the year. The petitioners observed that there was no island 'so little known or cared for, and none more oppressed' than Anguilla.

The petition, like that of 1825, went unheeded. In fact the plight of the Anguillians was made worse following the merger, in 1883, of the Presidency of St Kitts and the Presidency of Nevis. Consequently, a number of acts were repealed, one of the first being Act No 21 of 1825 which gave the freeholders in Anguilla the right to elect a representative to the House of Assembly in St Kitts. Also repealed were the various Vestry Acts: the day-to-day administration of the island was placed in the hands of a district magistrate.

The great famine

The nineteenth century closed with Anguillians once again in the grip of famine. A prolonged drought 'obliterated' all food crops and destroyed most of the cattle, sheep and pigs. So grave was the situation that out of a population of 4400 people around 3500 were given government assistance 'to save them from actual starvation'.

HERITAGE COLLECTION

Situated at Pond Ground in East End, the collection contains an array of Anguillian artefacts, old records and photographs which go back to the golden age of the Arawaks; the days when poverty bred invention; the revolutionary era. Founded and maintained by Colville Petty, the heritage collection opens history's window and allows a peek at the progression of a proud, resolute and industrious people.

| 11 |
Struggle for separation

At the beginning of the twentieth century Anguilla enjoyed a brief period of respite with the expansion of the cotton industry. In 1904 some 300 acres of land were under cultivation and exports reached a peak in the period 1910–1911 when 148,595 lbs were shipped abroad. However, during the First World War (1914–1918) exports were reduced to a mere trickle and shortly afterwards the entire cotton industry was wiped out by the boll weevil. In the ensuing economic depression Anguillian men and boys flocked to the Dominican Republic where they found employment in the sugar cane fields, and subsequently to the oil refineries of Aruba.

Constitutional reform

The depression of the 1920s and 1930s caused much discontent throughout the Caribbean and eventually resulted in labour disturbances in most of the islands, hastening constitutional reform and leading in 1936 to limited franchise being introduced in St Kitts, Nevis and Anguilla and permitting Anguillians to choose a representative to sit in the Legislative Council in St Kitts. A further development was the appointment of the Moyne Commission to study social conditions in the British West Indies. One of its principal recommendations was the granting of universal adult suffrage to all the territories, but it was not until 1952 that universal adult suffrage came into being in the Presidency of St Kitts, Nevis and Anguilla.

In 1956, with the dissolution of the Leeward Islands Federation, the Presidency was re-styled Colony and was granted a ministerial system of government. When the West Indies Federation was created two years later the Colony was included as a single unit.

The revolutionary period

Despite the various constitutional changes the Anguillian people remained powerless. In 1958, a petition was presented to the

64

Governor, Alexander Williams, asking him 'to bring about the dissolution of the ... political and administrative association of Anguilla with St Kitts'. The 3546 signatories warned the Governor that 'a people cannot live without hope for long without erupting socially'. The petition was ignored.

The West Indies Federation collapsed in 1962 and the British Government attempted a federation of the 'Little Eight' (Barbados and the Leeward and Windward Islands). When that failed they decided to grant the islands new constitutions to provide for statehood in association with Britain. The months preceding this saw the resurgence of Anguillian nationalism and a demand for separation from St Kitts. However the Associated State of St Kitts, Nevis and Anguilla was created on 27 February 1967 and the inclusion of Anguilla against the wishes of its people sparked off the Anguilla revolution.

Until 1967 Anguilla remained relatively poor and undeveloped, with no industries, no paved roads, no electricity, no pipe-borne water, no telephones and no proper port facilities. Health, sanitation and education facilities were grossly inadequate. The Anguillians placed full blame for their island's plight on the Government in St Kitts, holding that St Kitts took the lion's share of all development assistance to the colony to the detriment of the people of Anguilla and Nevis. What concretised that view was an allegation that at a political meeting in St Kitts, the Chief Minister, Robert Bradshaw, had threatened to turn Anguilla into a desert. Social conditions in Anguilla convinced its people that Bradshaw's threat was real and that they should break all constitutional links with St Kitts and forge direct ties with 'Mother England'. To most Anguillians statehood meant the strengthening of St Kitts' domination and stranglehold over their island and they concluded that if Anguilla was to progress its people had to take their destiny into their own hands. That is what they did under the leadership of Ronald Webster, Atlin Harrigan, Wallace Rey, Collins O. Hodge, Alfred Webster, John Rogers, Charlie Fleming and others.

The high point of the revolution occurred on Tuesday 30 May 1967 when a hostile crowd of Anguillians surrounded the police headquarters and expelled the thirteen-man contingent of St Kitts policemen who were stationed in Anguilla. The men were disarmed at Wallblake Airport and dispatched by air to St Kitts. Premier Bradshaw's response was swift. He declared a state of emergency, cut off all communications and trading links between Anguilla and St Kitts, pledging to re-establish law and order more firmly than ever in Anguilla and bring the culprits to justice. Meanwhile the Anguillians established a peacekeeping committee, under the chairmanship of Walter Hodge, to manage the island's affairs until elections could be held. The

Landsome House was occupied for many years by the Warden/Magistrate of Anguilla who was responsible for the management of the island's day to day affairs. It represented the seat of political power and was the reason why it was destroyed by fire on 8 March 1967 at the beginning of the Anguilla revolution. The house was built in the middle of the nineteenth century and belonged at that time to the Rey family. (THE LATE HUGH REY)

committee, which was wholly self-elected, comprised representatives of the various residential districts.

With a view to defending Anguilla's newly required freedom, the peacekeeping committee decided to launch a military attack on St Kitts, overthrow the Bradshaw Government and install one sympathetic to the Anguillian cause. To this end an eighteen-man party of mostly Anguillian young men and boys landed on the beach at Half Way Tree on St Kitts' southwest coast at 2 am on Saturday 10 June 1967. They were transported to Basseterre where they carried out attacks on the defence force camp, police headquarters and power station, but these fizzled out, partly because the promised support from Kittitians did not materialise. Nonetheless, the abortive coup provided the Anguillians with some protection because Bradshaw had to put his own house in order before trying to retake Anguilla.

On 11 July 1967 the peacekeeping committee held a plebiscite to determine the extent to which there was popular support for the revolution and thus secession from St Kitts. The result was an overwhelming vote (1813 to 5) in favour of secession and of establishing an interim government. A further step towards legitimising the island's status was the 'enactment' of a constitution which provided for a council of five elected and two nominated members.

As the Anguillians consolidated their revolution the Commonwealth Caribbean Governments of Barbados, Guyana, Jamaica and Trinidad and Tobago sought a peaceful resolution of the crisis by convening a meeting of all the interested parties in Barbados on 25 July 1967, but agreement on conditions for Anguilla's return to constitutional rule under St Kitts was countered by a show of widespread discontent in Anguilla. The impasse was broken in December 1967 when, through the mediation efforts of two British parliamentarians, Nigel Fisher and Donald Chapman, an agreement for an interim settlement was reached. Under the terms of the agreement a senior British official, Tony Lee, was appointed to 'exercise basic administrative authority' over Anguilla, in conjunction with the Anguilla Council, for a period of one year beginning 8 January 1968.

Towards the end of 1968 all endeavours at getting the Government of St Kitts and the Anguilla Council to agree on the terms for an extension of the interim settlement failed and the British official left Anguilla on 9 January 1969, a sad blow to the morale of the Anguillian people. This created a serious split in the Council between the moderates who wanted the British official to stay and the radicals who did not. The Council, under pressure from radicals like Ronald Webster, Wallace Rey and Collins O. Hodge, announced that a plebiscite would be held on 6 February 1969 to seek support for a republican constitution which would make the island an 'independent republic': the outcome was 1739 to 4 votes in favour.

British intervention

Ironically, that same day the Fifth Conference of Heads of Government of Commonwealth Caribbean Countries, held in Trinidad, called 'on the United Kingdom to take all necessary steps in collaboration with the Government of the State (of St Kitts, Nevis and Anguilla) to confirm the territorial integrity of St Kitts, Nevis and Anguilla'. As a consequence the British Government embarked on a further endeavour to find a solution to the crisis and on 11 March 1969 Junior Minister William Whitlock arrived in Anguilla with proposals for the establishment of an interim British administration headed by a commissioner. The proposals were unacceptable to the radicals in the Anguilla Council and they expelled Whitlock from the island within a few hours of his arrival. In response some 400 British troops

Royal Airforce plane transporting some of the British invasion force
(CLIVE CARTY)

invaded Anguilla on 19 March and established an administration under Commissioner Tony Lee, who was empowered to make provision for securing and maintaining public safety and order in Anguilla as part of the Associated State of St Kitts, Nevis and Anguilla.

The British Government now had an opportunity to look at a long-term solution to the crisis. A commission of inquiry was set up, under the chairmanship of Sir Hugh Wooding, to study the causes of the Anguilla problem and to make recommendations accordingly. The commission submitted its report in November 1970, one of its principal recommendations being that Anguilla should remain an integral part of the State of St Kitts, Nevis and Anguilla, but with increased representation in the House of Assembly. The report was rejected in its entirety by the Anguilla Council and people and the constitutional impasse continued.

Formal separation

The British Parliament eventually approved the Anguilla Act 1971 to enable the British Commissioner to provide a more effective administration in Anguilla. This course of action met with strong condemnation from several governments throughout the Caribbean. The

Anguilla Act and the Anguilla (Administration) Order of 1971 gave the Anguillians some measure of autonomy within the framework of the Associated State of St Kitts, Nevis and Anguilla.

Persistent agitation by the Anguilla Council for continuing constitutional advancement led to the Anguilla (Constitution) Order 1976 which provided for a ministerial system of government. When general elections under the new order were held on 15 March 1976 the

People's Progressive Party, led by Ronald Webster, won six of the seven seats and Ronald Webster became Anguilla's first Chief Minister. The fight for formal separation from St Kitts continued and Anguilla finally became a separate British Dependent Territory on 19 December 1980.

Ronald Webster – 'father of the Anguillian nation' (COLVILLE PETTY)

| 12 |

System of government and politics

Today Anguilla has a modified Westminster-style system of government. It has a Governor, an Executive Council and a House of Assembly. The constitution provides for the Governor to exercise, on behalf of Her Majesty, the executive authority of Anguilla and confers upon him the necessary powers to do so. He is required to consult with the Executive Council in the formulation of policy for consideration by the House of Assembly, the island's law-making body. The Chief Minister is the leader of government business in the Assembly and there is a Leader of the Opposition who is appointed by the Governor.

For the purpose of electing members to the House of Assembly, Anguilla is divided into seven electoral districts each of which elects one member. To be eligible for election a person must belong to Anguilla, be twenty-one years or over and be registered as a voter. All 'belongers' eighteen years and over have the right to vote.

Because the House of Assembly has a life of five years general elections are constitutionally due every five years. They may be held sooner if the Governor accepts the advice of the Chief Minister to dissolve the Assembly, or where a motion declaring a lack of confidence in the Government has been passed by the House of Assembly, in which case the Governor would set the date for general elections.

Anguilla has a multi-party political system. It has a first-past-the-post electoral system in which a candidate needs to get one vote more than his or her nearest rival to win a seat in the House of Assembly. Likewise, the party with the majority of seats, or which enters a coalition with another party in order to control the majority of seats, forms the government. The Anguillian people's confidence in the electoral process, their support for democratic principles and practices and their respect for individual freedoms and basic human rights mean that the transfer of political power on the island is peaceful. The execution of government business is undertaken by the civil service.

As regards the judiciary, Anguilla is a member of the Eastern Caribbean Supreme Court. Its law is the English common law supplemented by locally enacted legislation. The weekly magistrate's court

NATIONAL SONG

God Bless Anguilla
Nurture and keep her,
Noble and beauteous
She stands midst the sea.
O land of the happy
A haven we'll make thee
Our lives and love
We give unto thee.

Chorus
With heart and soul
We'll build our nation,
Proud, strong and free.
We'll love her, hold her
Dear to our hearts for eternity
Let truth and right our banner be
We'll march ever on.

Mighty we'll make her,
Long may she prosper,
God grant her leaders
Wisdom and grace.
May glory and honour,
Ever attend her,
Firm shall she stand
Throughout every age.

Alex Richardson

deals with minor offences and small claims, and there is also a high court presided over by a judge which the island shares with Montserrat, also a British Dependent Territory. It normally sits twice a year and its decisions are subject to review by the court of appeal. The Privy Council in England is the final court of appeal. Law and order are maintained by the highly disciplined Royal Anguilla Police Force but Anguillians are generally law-abiding and incidents of serious crime are rare.

| 13 |
The story of Anguilla's stamps

The story of Anguilla's postage stamps runs parallel to the island's constitutional and political history and provides a pictorial representation of a people's struggle for freedom and self-realisation.

Anguilla began issuing its own stamps only in the late 1960s, having been prevented from doing so for nearly a century by virtue of its status as a political appendage of St Kitts. Despite the legislative union established between them in 1825, Anguilla was absent from the first stamps released by the Presidency of St Kitts in 1870. In 1883 the Presidency of St Kitts and Anguilla and the Presidency of Nevis were joined to form the Presidency of St Kitts-Nevis. Their first combined stamp issues of 1903 were inscribed *ST KITTS-NEVIS*; Anguilla, the Cinderella, was once again omitted. As a consequence the stamps used in Anguilla, concurrently with the stamps of the Colony of the Leeward Islands, were those thus inscribed.

It was not until 1948 that Anguilla appeared on a postage stamp for the first time. That year a map of Anguilla, including Dog, Seal, Scrub and Anguillita islands, was depicted on two St Kitts-Nevis stamps, the ten shillings and one pound denominations. Its second appearance was on 10 November 1950 when the St Kitts Government released a set of overprints to commemorate the 300th anniversary of the English settlement of Anguilla. The set of six stamps, bearing the inscription *ST KITTS-NEVIS*, was overprinted with *ANGUILLA TERCENTENARY 1650–1950*.

In 1952, some 82 years after St Kitts had issued its first postage stamp, Anguilla appeared on a stamp as part of the title of the Presidency for the first time. As a result of constitutional reforms the 1952 definitives (comprising twelve stamps) carried the inscription *SAINT CHRISTOPHER NEVIS ANGUILLA*. The $1.20 East Caribbean (EC) dollar denomination depicted the salt pond at Road Bay (see Chapter 15, page 79).

It was only after the 1967 revolution that Anguilla began to issue its own postage stamps. Ironically, the first issue comprised the St Christopher, Nevis and Anguilla 1963 definitives from which the inscription *Saint Christopher Nevis Anguilla* was obliterated and replaced by the words *Independent Anguilla*. The work was undertaken by Island Press Inc. in St Thomas, United States Virgin Islands.

The stamps were released on 4 September 1967 and their historic value and relative scarcity eventually resulted in an astronomical rise in market value. (The selling price of a full set of sixteen, in mint condition, is around EC $30,000 at the time of going to press.)

The first definitive set of postage stamps ever issued by Anguilla went on sale on 27 November 1967 and the first commemorative set, which depicted Anguillian boats including the *Warspite* and the *Atlantic Star*, on 11 May 1968. The definitives were released in three batches and portrayed the Sombrero lighthouse, the mahogany tree, St Mary's Church, The Valley police station, an old plantation house at Mount Fortune, The Valley post office, the West End Methodist Church, Wallblake Airport, Sandy Ground, Island Harbour, a map of Anguilla, a hermit crab and starfish, a hibiscus, a spiny lobster and a local scene. Thereafter the definitives and several commemorative sets with the inscription *ANGUILLA* were released.

On 9 January 1969 Anguilla released a set of commemorative stamps as an assertion of the people's determination to be independent of St Kitts. The set comprised the 1967 definitives overprinted with *INDEPENDENCE JANUARY, 1969*. Some weeks later, when Anguilla was invaded by British forces (see Chapter 11, page 67) its unilateral declaration of independence came to an end. However, the island's stamps continued to bear the inscription *ANGUILLA*. The situation changed with the coming into force of the Anguilla Act and Anguilla (Administration) Order, both of 1971, which strengthened the Commissioner's control over the island's affairs. As a consequence the inscription *ANGUILLA* was removed from the postage stamps and replaced by *H. M. COMMISSIONER IN ANGUILLA* together with the royal cypher ER. The first commemorative stamps to bear this inscription were issued on 29 November 1971 and depicted paintings by some of the old masters, Raphael, Botticelli, Murillo and Dürer. The first *H. M. COMMISSIONER IN ANGUILLA* definitive issue was released in 1972 and highlighted various aspects of life in Anguilla.

When Anguilla was formally separated from the Associated State of St Kitts, Nevis and Anguilla on 19 December 1980 (see Chapter 11, page 00) the occasion was marked by a special set of stamps depicting the 1825 Petition for Separation, the ballot paper used in the 1967 referendum, the airport blockade (1967), the three dolphins flag and a celebration scene. The stamps were captioned *SEPARATION* from St Kitts. In addition, the 1977 definitives were overprinted with *SEPARATION 1980*. These two separation issues were the last stamps to be inscribed *H. M. COMMISSIONER IN ANGUILLA*. Since that time all stamps, commencing with the 1981 Easter issue, have carried the inscription *ANGUILLA*.

| 14 |
Anguilla's national flag

Until 1967, the only flag flown in Anguilla was the Union Jack of Great Britain. The 1967 revolution prompted the introduction of another flag, featuring two mermaids with a shell between them. This flag was sent by a group of Anguillians living in San Francisco and was hoisted when the Statehood flag was torn down. It was never really accepted and was soon replaced by the Three Dolphins flag, which immediately became popular and is still used by many people today, although unofficially. The three dolphins are coloured orange, to represent endurance, unity and strength, and are in a circle for continuity. The flag has a white background, for peace and tranquillity, with a turquoise-blue base representing the surrounding sea and also faith, youth and hope.

The Union Jack and the Three Dolphins flags were used for many years but there was a strong feeling that Anguilla should have its own official flag. A previous Governor of Anguilla, Mr Brian Canty, suggested a new flag and drew sketches which were sent to London for approval by Her Majesty the Queen. The new flag, which was first hoisted on 30 May 1990, is a blue ensign with a Union Jack in the top left corner and a shield on the right side which shows three orange dolphins on a white background with a turquoise-blue base. The design thus incorporates affiliation to Britain and the Anguilla Three Dolphins flag.

The governor's official flag comprises the Union Jack and the Anguilla coat of arms surrounded by a laurel wreath. It is flown at Government House when the Governor is in residence and on any motor car or boat in which he is making an official visit.

The coat of arms uses the same dolphin design that appears on the flag and is edged with gold. The official seal is the shield with a double circle around it containing the words *Anguilla: Strength and Endurance.*

The new Anguilla official flag

The Mermaid flag

The Three Dolphins flag

The Governor's official flag

Salt production in the early 1960s   (BRENDA CARTY)

Bagging salt for export   (BRENDA CARTY)

| 15 |
Industries of the past

Salt production

Salt production was an important source of revenue and employment in Anguilla from the early eighteenth century until as recently as 1985, salt being an essential but scarce commodity, much in demand both locally in the Caribbean and also in Europe.

The earliest report of salt production in Anguilla is in an old record of the Anguilla Council. A deposition made in 1769 by Jahabad Clarke, master of the brigantine *Elizabeth*, indicates that

> *On 23rd April he sailed from the island of Grenada bound for this island [Anguilla] for a load of salt. On 28th instant, turning up that shore, there being a small sandy bay off the harbour being enclosed with a parcel of shoals and shallow ground, and not being acquainted, the brigantine miss stays and sailed on the reef, was immediately bilged and found it was impossible to get her off...*

In the early days the salt producing ponds were regarded as common property; labourers would collect the salt on specified days for their employers and then when official reaping stopped at 2 pm they could collect for themselves. It was common therefore to see numerous piles of salt along the shores of the ponds, some belonging to the big landowners and others to their workers or to free individuals. There would then be movements of salt as purchases and sales were made, but most of the salt was eventually exported.

In 1855 the Anguilla Salt Ponds Joint Stock Company was formed and a lease granted to operate the Road Salt Pond; from that time royalties were paid but in this case they were set too high and the company failed. However, salt was reaped nearly every year from one or more of the ponds and the royalties paid proved an important source of revenue. In 1868 the pond was leased to Edward Lake Carter who harvested salt for ten years. On his death the lease was passed on to his daughter, who married Wager Rey from St Martin. Management of the Road Pond stayed in the Rey family for many years, and was a successful operation. Wager Rey built dams around

The pump house – Road Bay Salt Company   (ANDRIOLA/CARTY)

the pond to prevent rainwater flowing into the salt-making area and a long middle dam to provide an adequate holding and settling area for sea water. Later a floodgate area was built for the loaded flats. His son, Carter Rey, installed the first diesel-driven pump and the mill for grinding coarse salt into fine.

After a few years of failure in the 1950s, salt production flourished again. Long Pond in Sandy Hill produced small quantities of salt until the 1960s and at West End Pond salt was reaped in 1963 and 1974. However, the main producing pond remained the 240-acre Road Salt Pond at Sandy Ground, leased from the government by the Anguilla Road Salt Company through Joseph Owen and later, Rupert Carty. Exports were good and regular: four hundred tons of salt were shipped monthly to Texaco in Trinidad for use in the oil industry and fairly large exports went to Guadeloupe, Puerto Rico and Barbados. Many of the islands took smaller amounts of fine salt, ground at Sandy Ground. Successful reaping continued until 1985, when the devaluation of the Trinidad and Tobago dollar rendered it uneconomic.

Reaping

Salt formed at the bottom of the ponds by evaporation and a good crop was dependent upon dry sunny days to complete the evaporation process. In order to reap the salt, crews of four to six men and women would wade into the pond, poling a large flat-bottomed wooden boat called a 'flat'. A cake of salt was brought to the surface with gloved hands, rinsed in a basket and thrown into the flat, where it broke into various sizes of crystal. When full each flat was taken to the edge of the pond and the salt loaded into barrels, where it was taken on a concrete ramp to the salt heap and left to be shipped or taken to the factory to be ground into fine salt. The salt house or pump house has now been renovated and converted into a bar and restaurant where it is still possible to see some of the old machinery (see Chapter 17, page 98). In recent years use was made of a front-end loader to move the salt. At one time the workers carried the salt in boxes on their heads and it was then emptied into barrels to be measured. Each flat held about eighteen barrels of salt and weighed 300 pounds. The months of reaping were usually mid-July to September, dependent upon the amount of rainfall, which could delay reaping by slowing down the evaporation process, sometimes spoiling the crop. About 200 workers were usually employed at Road Salt Pond for the reaping, which could take up to thirty days to complete and produced 7000–8000 tons of salt.

A revival of the salt industry seems unlikely, although as can be seen in the drier months, salt still forms. A demonstration of the reaping sometimes takes place during the Cultural and Educational Festival (see Chapter 6, page 23) and it is always an interesting event. In the meantime, the ponds are an attraction to nature lovers as they provide a habitat for many ducks, herons and other birds.

Phosphate mining on Sombrero

Sombrero is an arid island, its volcanic base and limestone capping rising in cliffs from twenty to forty feet (6–12 m) above sea-level. It has no soil and no beaches. Nevertheless, it has been of considerable, if brief, importance to the economy of Anguilla by virtue of significant deposits of phosphate of lime, discovered during a geological survey in 1810.

Originally quarried by American speculators, the island became the subject of an ownership dispute between the United States and Britain, which was eventually resolved in Britain's favour and in 1865 a twenty-one year lease was granted to the Sombrero Phosphate Company at an annual rent of £1000. Extensive mining facilities were established on the island, including a light steam railway, a steam

Flats for collecting the salt *overleaf*   (MICHAEL BOURNE)

Silent witness to one of those who died on Sombrero   (COLVILLE PETTY)

rock crusher and accommodation for the workers. The work force comprised many Anguillians, who went there, especially in times of prolonged drought and famine, to supplement their meagre incomes and provide for their families. Still evident are the graves of some who died there, hewn out of rock and covered with the excavated stone because of the absence of soil. Within a few years of its operations the Phosphate Company experienced financial difficulties due to the rapid depletion of the phosphate deposits. By the late 1860s the phosphate, which lay in pockets twenty to thirty feet deep, could only be extracted by blasting, adding to the already high cost of production and proving a severe drain on the resources of the company, which was forced into liquidation in 1871.

The remainder of the lease was purchased by a syndicate in London who paid the liquidator £55 000. However it soon realized that the venture would not be a profitable one and set up a joint-stock company, called the New Sombrero Phosphate Company, to which it sold the lease for £110 000. When the shareholders of the new company found out that they had been conned by the deal they took the matter to court and it eventually reached the House of Lords which found in their favour.

Phosphate mining on Sombrero had petered out by 1890. The chimney of the boiler-house is still standing but the many storms which have ravaged the island over the years have levelled the phosphate labourers' living quarters.

84

Remains of the boiler-house on Sombrero   (Colville Petty)

Sombrero – accessible only by steep ladder in calm seas   (Colville Petty)

| PART III |

Exploring Anguilla

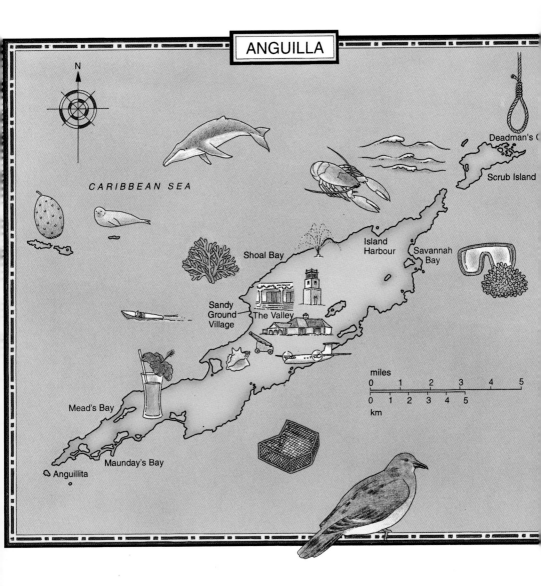

ANGUILLA

N

CARIBBEAN SEA

Shoal Bay

Island
Harbour

Savannah
Bay

Deadman's C

Scrub Island

Sandy
Ground
Village

The Valley

Mead's Bay

Maunday's Bay

Anguillita

miles
0   1   2   3   4   5

0   1   2   3   4   5
km

| 16 |
The Valley

Sprawled over a wide area in the central part of Anguilla is The Valley, the largest concentration of population on the island, although by most standards it can hardly be called a town. All of Anguilla's main administrative offices are to be found here, including the Government Secretariat and ministerial buildings, the Treasury, the offshore finance and company registry, the customs headquarters, the lands and survey office, the police station, the magistrate's and registrar's offices, the court house and the prison. Two outstanding new buildings are the post office, completed in 1994, and the library and resource centre, completed the following year. Both were designed by British architect David Kenworthy. Further north from the post office is the Cable and Wireless office, the Caribbean Commercial Bank, and the Anglican church of **St Mary's**, which is a simple but

The bell tower of St Mary's Anglican Church   (ANDRIOLA/CARTY)

Governor Shave issues a sporting challenge to Ras Bucket in Webster Park
(MICHAEL BOURNE)

interesting building. The present church was completed in 1967 and is on the site of the original wooden church built in the latter part of the nineteenth century.

The **Anguilla Museum**, on the road leading east from St Mary's, was opened in 1996 and contains many interesting artifacts and information on Anguilla's history. The office of the Anguilla National Trust is in the same building. Historical information is available also in the heritage room of the library and resource centre. The nearby **Landsome Bowl and Cultural Centre** is now an auditorium for carnival and other events. At one time there was a house here for the warden from St Kitts. He was the authority in charge and lived at Landsome Estate until the 1967 revolution, when the house was burnt down; luckily he escaped.

The road to the hospital is **Queen Elizabeth Avenue**, so named in commemoration of the visit of HM Queen Elizabeth II in 1994. The fine display of **ficus benjamina** trees along the road were planted by the Anguilla Beautification Club, a group which has helped to plant many areas on the island (see Chapter 7, page 28). **Webster Park** can be found here, named after Ronald Webster who led the people during the revolution of 1967 (see Chapter 11, page 64), and later became the Chief Minister of Anguilla under the new constitution. The park is used for many sporting events throughout the year, (see

Chapter 6, page 24) and first-class cricket matches are played there. Queen Elizabeth Avenue leads to **The Princess Alexandra Hospital**, opened in 1993 and of a good size for Anguilla's population. Princess Alexandra laid the foundation stone.

A drive or walk west from the traffic lights at the beginning of Queen Elizabeth Avenue will take you to Lower Valley, the older part of The Valley. The **Ebenezer Methodist Church** on the left is the oldest church in Anguilla. The rectangular stone building, with gothic arched windows, a pitched pine roof and a belfry, is still used for worship. Further along on the right are several small charming houses built in the late nineteenth and early twentieth century which have been extremely well maintained and painted in attractive colours. Two of these homes belong to the Hodge family (see Chapter 11, page 65). The stone house was apparently built by one of the many Dutch families who resided here during the latter half of the last century, a fact borne out by its distinctive design. Dutch names such as Vanterpool and Heyliger are still common on the island. Note the shingle roof on the adjacent wooden house.

On the left of the road is **Koal Keel restaurant**, an old plantation house used as a residence for island officials for many years. It is well

Koal Keel Restaurant – just the place to relax for a while
(MICHAEL BOURNE)

worth a visit since upstairs you can sit in pleasant surroundings and enjoy breakfast, coffee or bakery items at any time of the day. The original house was constructed in the late 1700s and was one of the main buildings of a relatively large sugar estate. The first floor was made of stone and the upper floor of wood. You can still see the large blocks of stone and the renovated brick oven (see Chapter 4, page 15).

PRESERVATION FOR GENERATIONS

The Anguilla National Trust, whose motto appears above, was established in 1993 to oversee the preservation and management of the island's cultural heritage: its historic buildings, places of natural interest or beauty and wetlands. It is a statutory body concerned with the preservation of furniture, pictures, documents and artefacts of any description having national, historical, artistic or cultural interest.

Some of the major projects in which it is engaged include the development of the Anguilla National Museum, the Big Spring at Island Harbour and the Fountain National Park and Cavern. This ecologically diverse and archaeologically significant site will become part of a system of parks and protected areas to be managed by the Trust.

The old hospital building is on the right, but if you turn left and go up the hill you reach the old court house. All that remains of this once prominent building at **Crocus Hill** is the stone basement, constructed in the eighteenth century and used as a powder magazine for storing weapons and explosives. It was later converted into a prison, although apparently not a very secure one: on the night of 13 December 1831 three men, under sentence of death, escaped by cutting their way through the roof. Prison conditions in the late nineteenth century were so deplorable that a woman hanged herself on the first night she was there and a government official of the time described it as a 'most miserable and disgusting dungeon'. This was also the view of Anguillians when they petitioned Queen Victoria in 1872 for separation from St Kitts (see Chapter 10, page 62). They complained: 'The old slavery dungeon now used as a gaol ... has been condemned ... as a place unfit for the reception of humans'. The old court house was destroyed by *Hurricane Alice* in 1955, although the small cells and a stone-walled enclosure, topped with broken bottles, are still intact. The wooden upper floor was once the court, treasury, post office and customs, thus forming the centre of government business at one time.

At Crocus Hill you can also see the new reservoir which has a capacity of 500,000 gallons and holds the water pumped from the wells lower down in The Valley, behind the Agricultural Department. The water is treated and sent by gravity to all parts of the island through pipes of four to ten inches, the larger size enabling the water to reach everywhere without the necessity of pumping (see Chapter 3, page 9).

On the southern outskirts of The Valley, near the airport roundabout, are **Wallblake House** and **St Gerard's Church. Wallblake House** is one of Anguilla's few historical houses, standing on six acres of land. The house is believed to have been built in the late eighteenth century by a sugar planter named Valentine Blake, its name having changed to Wallblake with usage. It was one of the leading residences on the island and was a plantation house for the Wallblake estate. A brick in the old bakery still shows the original date of 1787. The foundations and cistern are built of cut stone which came from East End or Scrub Island. They are held together with lime made from burnt corals and shells mixed with molasses and marl. The house has a wooden roof and attractive tray ceilings with beading and decorative woodwork.

In the early twentieth century the house belonged to the Rey family and the surrounding estates, mostly of cotton, were managed from there. This influential planter family, which included Carter Rey and Frank Rey, dominated economic and social activity on the island until the 1950s (see Chapter 15, page 79). When they died Wallblake House was passed to their sister, Marie Lake, who died in 1965 and willed the house and lands to the Roman Catholic Church. For some time the

Wallblake House – a landmark for over 200 years
(MICHAEL BOURNE)

house was used for services but eventually **St Gerard's Church** was built in the grounds and dedicated in 1966. The church is a simple but unusual one, making excellent use of multicoloured local stones, pebbles, tiles and wood. There is open brickwork at the sides and a beautiful stone altar. Father John Strychers, a Belgian priest, was the inspiration behind this church and was the architect, supervisor, electrician and carpenter for much of the work.

During the tourist season from December to April the Anguilla Archaeological and Historical Society arranges tours of Wallblake House and several other houses in The Valley.

On the opposite side of the road is the old **Factory** building which has now been converted into an ice-cream parlour. The building was called the Factory because it housed the island's only cotton ginnery where the cleaning and baling of locally grown cotton was undertaken in preparation for shipping to England via St Kitts. The machinery has been preserved and can still be seen inside the shop. The tourism office is upstairs in this building.

Interior view of the distinctive St Gerard's Church *opposite*
(MICHAEL BOURNE)

The present airport, completed in 1988 and opened by Princess Alexandra
(ANDRIOLA/CARTY)

The Factory was once the centre of all trading and commercial activity in Anguilla and served as a general store which sold groceries, hardware items, clothing and just about everything that people needed. A variety of other services were included, one of which was a barter system whereby people could obtain goods on credit and pay for them in cotton. There was a banking service which allowed Anguillians who received cheques from overseas to cash them. There were no banks on the island at that time so it was a vital service. The Factory also provided insurance, travel arrangements and even built coffins.

Wallblake Airport has grown from nothing more than a grassy strip in 1966 to a busy airport with over 4000 passengers arriving monthly. The airport first began operations in 1941, during the Second World War, when a strip was cleared by the Americans for use in emergency landings. The grass strip remained until 1967, when paving was begun and in 1968 110 feet (34 m) of the paved section came into use. It was not until 1974 that the entire runway of 3600 feet (1097 m) was completely surfaced.

Scheduled flights to Anguilla began in 1956, with Leeward Islands Air Transport (LIAT) being the first regular carrier. In 1978 Windward Islands Airways (WINAIR) began a scheduled service, followed in 1984 by Air BVI and in 1987 by American Eagle. Night flights started in February 1983 when the lighting system was commissioned.

Charter flights have always been important and Tyden Air and Air Anguilla run charters, with as many as thirty flights daily (see Chapter 24, page 135).

The present airport building was designed by Design Collaboratives International, based in Barbados, and built by Ace Contractors of Anguilla. The fifty-foot control tower was added in 1990.

The Valley has one hotel, **Lloyds Hotel**, used mainly by business visitors. It is five minutes' walk from Crocus Bay and one and a quarter miles from the airport.

Beaches near The Valley

Crocus Bay, at the bottom of the steep concrete road from the Lower Valley Road, is a fishing centre and also has a good beach for swimming and snorkelling. There is a popular restaurant and bar on this beach, **Roy's Place**.

Little Bay can best be reached by boat, but the adventurous can enjoy a climb down the cliffs with the aid of a rope. You are well rewarded as the beach is quite secluded and very attractive. It is an excellent place to snorkel for it is within the Marine Park area (see Chapter 9, page 51) and is a nursery for many fish. Schools of fish and some quite large fish are generally seen at the base of the cliffs.

Further along the same road is **Limestone Bay**. This is another secluded beach but the sea can be quite rough, with a current at times, so care is needed. On calm days it is also very good for snorkelling.

On the south coast of the island, **Forest Bay** was once an important trading port used by many schooners and sloops. In the 1930s and until 1948 there was a customs building at the Forest. It is not a particularly good beach to visit but what is lacking on the surface is made up for under the sea where there are some interesting seaweed beds and reefs. **Smugglers Restaurant** is here.

Little Harbour is completely enclosed by a reef and consequently makes excellent safe anchorage in times of storms or hurricanes. The shallow water means it is very safe for learning to windsurf or sail and it is a good beach for children. At the back of the beach is a pond which has lots of mangroves (see Chapter 7, page 28) and considerable bird life. The **Cinnamon Reef Beach Club** is situated here.

Between Forest Bay and Little Harbour is **Corito**. It is not very suitable for swimming or relaxing as there is only a narrow strip of sand but the coast is good for walking and there is a pond with ducks, herons and other bird life.

| 17 |

Sandy Ground and North Hill

Sandy Ground is an interesting village between the Road Bay and the salt pond and has much to offer to visitors. Approaching the village you will see the Road Salt Pond (see Chapter 15, page 79) on your right. Drive alongside the pond until you come to the buildings that were used for grinding the salt, one of which has been converted into a late-night bar. Inside are displays giving some of the history of salt production, and some of the grinding machinery is still there. The four wooden buildings comprised the salt factory complex and were the centre of operations for the industry for over 100 years. The grinding and bagging took place in the main building with the triple pitched roof, and some of the fine salt was stored here until it could be exported. If you are feeling energetic you can walk right round the pond and your efforts will be rewarded by the abundant birdlife here (see Chapter 8, page 40).

Nearby on the opposite side of the road is The Dive Shop (see Chapter 9, page 45), should you be interested in scuba diving. A walk from here northwards along the beach will take you through the fishing village. The fishermen here supply many of the hotels and restaurants with lobsters, yellow tailed snapper, local dolphin, grouper and trigger fish. This is also one of the few places on the island where conchs are still caught. In general fishermen use pots or traps for their catches, although some troll with a rod and line.

At the northern end of the beach you will find the home of **Ivor the Diver**. He is well-known for the number of shells he has collected and he is sometimes willing to sell them. Beyond his house he has built into a wall some fifty feet (15 m) long by ten feet (3 m) high the many conch shells he has dived for over the years.

Another walk, this time heading south from the dive shop, will take you to **Johnno's Beach Bar and Restaurant**, popular for its regular dancing to the music of Dumpa on the steel pan, and other musical groups (see Chapter 4, page 15). There are several restaurants offering lunch and dinner along the beach at Sandy Ground. These are very popular, especially with the many yachtsmen who

Sandy Ground, with Road Salt Pond in the background (ANDRIOLA/CARTY)

Dance the night away at Johnno's Beach Bar (ANDRIOLA/CARTY)

The ninety year old White House (ANDRIOLA/CARTY)

anchor in the harbour, and offer excellent Caribbean and international dishes.

Directly behind Johnno's, on the pondside, is the **White House**. This belongs to Sir Emile Gumbs who was Chief Minister of Anguilla for thirteen years and in politics from the time of the Anguilla revolution, (see Chapter 11, page 64) until he retired in 1994. The house is a good example of vernacular architecture, with cut stone in the foundations, the upstairs built of wood, a pitched roof, shingles, and decorative railings and fretwork (see Chapter 4, page 11). The cut stone in the ground floor was brought from Sombrero. The ground floor of the house was used as a customs office during the time when the original owner, John Frederick Gumbs, Sir Emile's grandfather, was a customs officer.

The building next to Johnno's is the **police marine base** and present-day **customs office**. It was completed in 1991 and was designed to blend with the Caribbean-style housing on the beach. Here private boats arriving at Sandy Ground have to report to customs and obtain cruising and mooring permits if they wish to sail to other beaches in Anguilla (see Chapter 9, page 51). From the nearby police jetty you can get a boat to Sandy Island, about two miles offshore (see Chapter 24, page 135). Sandy Ground is the main port in Anguilla for the importation of goods from the other Caribbean islands, Puerto

Rico, the USA and the UK, and the commercial jetty is usually very busy. A range of vessels can usually be seen from small inter-island sloops to large container vessels and these provide some good photo-opportunities.

At the southern end of the beach you will come across the **Mariners Hotel**, with attractive Caribbean-style villas set among the sea grape trees directly on the beach. The hotel has its own sea-view restaurant, tennis court and swimming pool. Watersports equipment is available for hire. Nearby you can also arrange a cruise aboard the catamaran *Chocolat* to Sandy Island, Prickly Pear and other offshore cays. Sunset cruises are especially popular.

On the drive out from Sandy Ground eastwards, after you leave the pond area, you will see the **Mission House** on the right-hand side of the road. Originally a plantation house for the Road Estate where sugar and cotton were grown, it is believed to have been built in the nineteenth century. It was bought by the Methodist church in the early nineteenth century and served as the manse for many years. It is still owned by the church but rented privately now.

The village of **North Hill**, located one mile from the main road, has changed very little in recent years. When you reach the village, follow the road past the small church and keep driving; this will take you right to the point at the northern end of the **Road Bay** harbour. Early

The commercial jetty at Sandy Ground (ANDRIOLA/CARTY)

101

in the twentieth century there were several wooden buildings on the flat rocks at the point which were used as quarantine centres. It is probably more enjoyable to walk on this road as there are good views of Sandy Island to the west and Crocus Bay and Little Bay to the north-east.

Directly below the cliff, and especially visible in the morning, is an area in the sea which is particularly clear of rocks and is known locally as the **Blue Hole**. It is possible to walk down the steep path to the rocky beach, where many different types of coral are piled. It is also a good area for finding fossil shells and Blue Hole is a clear sandy area for swimming. A walk along the beach to the west leads to the remains of an old sugar mill, where parts of the boiling house and curing house can still be seen. The animal round is also still there. This is where the donkeys, mules or cattle were hitched to an axle and made to walk round and round turning the mills to crush the juice from cane stalks pushed by hand into the mills as they turned. It is not easy to find this area so unless you are adventurous you may need to ask someone to show you the way.

Returning to the village, there is another road that leads to a cliff overlooking **Katouche Bay**, where a walk down a steep path leads to the sea. The name probably derives from the De la Touche who led the French invasion of Anguilla in 1745 (see Chapter 10, page 59). On the ordnance survey map the bay is marked La Touche, but it has never been called that locally. There are manchineel trees along the beach which are poisonous (see Chapters 7 and 9, pages 28 and 50).

For another walk to the beach, drive back along the **North Hill Road** to the main road and turn left. At the first set of traffic lights turn left again. This road will take you past the **Governor's Residence** at **Old Ta**. The house was completed in 1973 and at that time was occupied by a commissioner from Britain. In 1982, Charles

Godden was sworn in as the first Governor of Anguilla and the house has been occupied by the Governor, who is the Queen's representative, since that time. The many attractive trees and plants in the gardens have name plaques put there by Governor and Mrs Shave, who were very interested in gardening and planted both at Government House and throughout the island. There are two guns in the grounds; one was found at Crocus Bay and the other at South Hill, where the Bethel Methodist Church now stands. Both guns are British naval cannons dating from the seventeenth century. Visitors may sign the book which is kept outside the Governor's Office.

Continue for a few yards and park in a field at the end of the road, just past the house. Walk north to the edge of the bush line for about 200 yards and then west until you reach a clear path going northwards, again about 200 yards. Follow this rocky path for about ten minutes until you see some large grey rocks to your left. Continue for a few more yards and follow the path down to the entrance of the **Gavannagh Cave**. The cave is a natural one which was mined for phosphate in the late nineteenth century. Walking into the cave is easy and if you take a flashlight you will be able to illuminate some of the corners and see the interesting roots that make their way deep into the cave from the tree in the centre. You can also see bats. It is believed that the Gavannagh Cave was the source of a cargo of phosphate, shipped from Anguilla to the USA in 1868, in which the fossilised remains of a large rodent known as *Amblyrhiza* were identified. More recently remains have been found at the Pitchapple Cave near North Side Road. The extinct rodent was unique to Anguilla, St Martin and St Barths and is called locally the 'giant rat', which is in fact a misnomer since it is believed to have been more like a guinea pig, agouti or chinchilla. However, giant it really was with an estimated length of six and a half feet (2 m) and weight of 330 lb (150 kg).

To continue to Katouche Bay, follow the path down, passing some tall cacti, through an attractive wooded area with lots of bromeliads or air plants on the trees. As you approach the sea there is an old well on your left; this whole area was once used for agriculture, hence the need for a water supply. The walk from the cave to the sea takes about twenty minutes at a fairly gentle pace and is recommended as a pleasant walk early in the morning or in the late afternoon.

Visitors to the area can stay at the private and secluded **Masara Resort**, which has thirteen one- or two-bedroomed apartments. The beach is just one or two minutes' walk away.

| 18 |

South Hill, Blowing Point and Rendezvous Bay

The **Bethel Methodist Church** at **South Hill** occupies an imposing position overlooking Sandy Ground. The stone structure, with buttresses supporting most of the walls, has Gothic arched windows and doors. The front of the building shows a white star below the bell-tower and above the two entrance doors. The roof underwent major repairs after it was partially destroyed by *Hurricane Donna* which struck Anguilla in 1960, and again after *Hurricane Luis* in 1995.

Blowing Point is a small but sprawling village with a surprisingly large number of inhabitants. It is the second most important port after Sandy Ground, being the nearest port to St Martin (see Chapter 23, page 127). There is a small police station, well-placed to spot any boats in difficulties in the channel.

The beach east of the jetty is used mostly by fishermen, who often take their catch to St Martin to sell, whilst the long sand spit to the west offers good safe bathing with several small pools which are ideal for children. The spit leads to a small outcrop of reef, good for walking and exploring. The nearby **Ferry Boat Inn** offers comfortable and spacious apartment accommodation with lovely views of St Martin. A further ten apartments and a two-bedroomed penthouse are available at **The Pavilion**, just two minutes' walk from the beach.

To the west of Blowing Point is **Rendezvous Bay**, a two-mile long stretch of white sand beach, good for shell collectors, with calm blue waters and a magnificent view of St Martin. The bay was the site of an Amerindian settlement and a large Arawak house was found here (see Chapter 10, page 57). A carbonised house post recovered here was dated about the late sixth century and several almost complete ceramic vessels, carved stone idols, pottery and tools have also been found. At the eastern end of Rendezvous Bay and accessible from Blowing Point is Anguilla's second-oldest hotel, the **Rendezvous**, which remains popular because of its friendly service and relaxed atmosphere. There are thirty rooms with single, double or villa accommodation among the trees.

First stop back on the main road to the west should be **The Great House**, which is well signposted about one and three quarter miles

Built in 1878, the main structure of Bethel Methodist Church remains much as it was (ANDRIOLA/CARTY)

from the traffic lights. Accommodation consists of twenty-seven rooms in Caribbean-style villas. This is an ideal spot for watersports and you can hire a windsurfer, kayak or sunfish sailboat and enjoy the strong breeze out in the bay.

Further west from The Great House is the **Sonesta Beach Resort**, chosen for the one-night stay of HM Queen Elizabeth II when she

Rendezvous Bay *overleaf* (ANDRIOLA/CARTY)

RESTAURANTS IN
SOUTH HILL, BLOWING POINT
AND RENDEZVOUS BAY

Aquarium
Short Curve
Ferry Boat Inn
Arlos
Lucy's Harbour View
The Great House
Sonesta Beach Resort

visited the island in 1994. The resort is well worth a visit and can be reached either by walking along the beach or by a drive along the main road. This western end of Rendezvous Bay is called **Merrywing Bay**. The Sonesta Beach has ninety rooms and the Moroccan influence in its architecture is unusual for a Caribbean resort. The archways and fine mosaic carving in the entrance way are genuine and were cut by craftsmen from Morocco. It is possible to arrange to spend a day here using all the sports facilities, including tennis courts, a well-equipped gymnasium and a large pool adjacent to the beach. Near the pool is a grill for snacks and lunches, and the resort also has a full restaurant. Sailboats, windsurfers and snorkelling gear are available, the beach here being particularly good for snorkelling. There are fine views of St Martin's mountains across the channel.

Paradise Cove is on the road to Sonesta Beach Resort; it is about a three-minute walk from Cove Bay. There are fourteen self-catering units set among tropical flowers and shrubs, with a large pool and terrace.

| 19 |
The West

The next port of call travelling westwards is **Cove Bay**, reached from the road marked to the Sonesta Beach Resort. Instead of turning left to Sonesta Beach, continue straight towards the sea. This lovely bay has calm waters and a virtually deserted beach, over one mile in length, with dunes behind. It is especially good for swimming and walking. Continue your drive along the sandy road beside **Cove Pond**. This was never used for salt production, although at one time a considerable amount of dredging was done as there were plans to build a marina. The root structures of mangrove trees growing here are open to the sea and make excellent nurseries for fish and other marine life. They are also popular nesting places for the pond and sea birds. (See Chapter 7, page 28).

You will now come to **Cap Juluca Hotel**. There are ninety-eight rooms here, including luxury double rooms, one- and two- bedroomed

Situated in 175 acres, the Cap Juluca Hotel skirts the calm turquoise reef-protected waters of Maunday's Bay   (MICHAEL BOURNE)

Shoal Bay West   (ANDRIOLA/CARTY)

suites and three- or four- bedroomed villas, and at the water's edge are two restaurants, **Chattertons** and **Pimms**, together with a beach bar which serves snacks. Other facilities at the Moorish-style hotel resort include a swimming pool, croquet and tennis courts and water-sports. You can walk along the sand or drive behind the villas, admiring the successful landscaping, to the far end of the beach, where there is another pond surrounded by attractive mangrove trees. Whilst quite common in Anguilla, the mangroves here are particularly lush. Return to the main entrance of the hotel and leave Cap Juluca by the road across Cove Pond, where you can see several pond birds, including the snowy egret, the black-necked stilt and the lesser yellowlegs, and often some sea birds as well (see Chapter 8, page 40).

Continue west along the main road for one mile and turn left alongside **West End Pond**. Once used for salt production, it was never as productive as Sandy Ground pond and the last time salt was reaped here was in 1974 (see Chapter 15, page 80). The road leads on to **Shoal Bay West**, a good spot for snorkelling. From the beach you can see Anguillita, the small island at the western tip of Anguilla, and there are excellent views too of St Martin. Look out for **Blowing Rock**: if you are there when the sea is rough you will see a spiral of water pushing through here at regular intervals. Stop for lunch or dinner at **Paradise Cafe**, where the food is delicious.

Cove Castles Resort   (ANDRIOLA/CARTY)

There are several villa complexes on this beach. **Cove Castles** is an elegant modern complex with twelve spacious and well-furnished units for two to six people. It is good for watersports and tennis and has its own boutique and restaurant. **Blue Waters Beach Apartments** are especially private and peaceful and are directly on the beach, overlooking the sea. Each apartment has a daily maid service and well-equipped kitchen, and the Paradise Cafe is nearby.

You have now completed the drive along the south side of the western section of the island. Return to the main road and this time, about one mile along on the left, turn into **Meta Resort of Anguilla**, delightfully situated on the point between Barnes Bay and Mead's

Blue Waters Beach Apartments   (ANDRIOLA/CARTY)

111

Mead's Bay   (BRENDA CARTY)

Bay. Its fifty-one rooms are spread along the beach, which offers excellent snorkelling off the rocks when the sea is reasonably calm. The hotel's pool and bar area is attractively laid out for relaxing and drinking and there are small pools with fish and lobster swimming around. This health resort has many facilities geared to the maintenance of fitness.

On leaving Meta Resort, take the first road to the left off the main road and follow it along the pondside into **Mead's Bay** with its exquisite mile-long beach of soft white sand. Here Anguilla's most sophisticated hotel, the **Malliouhana**, sits on a bluff overlooking two beautiful beaches. Its high ceilings, white walls, lobby fountain, Haitian prints and lush tropical gardens give an air of luxury and the restaurant is especially elegant. Most of the fifty-three rooms and suites overlook the sea and facilities include three pools, an exercise room, watersports, lighted tennis courts, boutique and boat service.

Two minutes' walk from the bay is **La Sirena Hotel**, decorated in typical Caribbean style. There are two freshwater pools, a tropical garden, bar, boutique and free use of snorkelling equipment. The restaurant serves West Indian and international cuisine.

If self-catering is more your style, try **Carimar Beach Club**, a first-class resort with twenty-three mainly two-bedroomed apartments with maid service and fully equipped kitchens. Tennis courts are on site

RESTAURANTS IN THE WEST

Pimms/Chattertons
Paradise Cafe
Cove Castles
West End-by-the Sea
Mango's
Meta Resort of Anguilla
Top of the Palms (La Sirena)
Frangipani Beach Club
Blanchards
Malliouhana

and there is a good restaurant, **Blanchards**, within one or two minutes' walk. **Frangipani Beach Club** is a relatively new complex decorated in Spanish style with fifteen units of one or two bedrooms and a penthouse suite.

Leaving Mead's Bay, the road leads through **Long Bay village** and back to the main road. After passing **South Hill Plaza**, a good stopping place for a meal, snack or souvenirs, look out for a paved road on the left about half a mile further on. This one-way road has beautiful views of Sandy Ground, Sandy Island, and the Road Pond, with North Hill and Shannon Hill on the opposite side.

Frangipani Beach Club (ANDRIOLA/CARTY)

| 20 |

Shoal Bay and Island Harbour

No visit to Anguilla is complete without a trip north to **Shoal Bay**; many say it has the best beach on the island, or even in the Caribbean. Follow Queen Elizabeth Avenue from The Valley, turn on to the main road and after about a mile there is a junction on the left clearly marked Shoal Bay.

On arrival at Shoal Bay you can settle down for a relaxing day, taking advantage of facilities more rarely found at other beaches. You can rent chairs, mats, snorkelling equipment or small paddle boats and lock-up facilities are available. Alternatively you can view the reef in a glass-bottomed boat or go out on a fishing trip, but it is advisable to book a fishing boat a day in advance either at the beach, or through one of the hotels. Reefs close to the shore provide shallow safe water for the beginner at snorkelling, whilst the more experienced can venture further out to other reefs. The clear blue water is delightful for swimming and is usually very safe. There are several places to eat at Shoal Bay, including **Uncle Ernie's**, where barbecued chicken, ribs or fish are specialities. **Reefside restaurant**, **Round Rock** and **Madeariman Reef** have a wide selection for lunch and dinner. **Serenity restaurant** is further along the beach to the north-east.

A walk along the beach here pays dividends, with views of Scrub Island and the coast along to Island Harbour as you round the point. If you decide to go west, another pleasant walk leads to **La Fontana** restaurant at the far end. Not far from La Fontana is **Fountain Cavern**, which is one of the most interesting caves in Anguilla and of great archaeological significance. The cave was the ceremonial centre for Arawaks, the earliest known inhabitants of Anguilla (see Chapter 10, page 57): evidence of their use of the cave includes a large stalagmite carved with the features of the Arawak Creator Deity, *Jocahu*, and a number of petroglyphs (rock carvings) have been found. The Fountain got its name from three crystal-clear pools of potable water, located deep in the interior, which tradition says were the source of water for most wells in Anguilla. Until the early 1950s, when a steel ladder was installed, entry to the cave was made by climbing down some thirty feet on the roots of a pitchapple tree. Currently a National Park is being developed on the land surrounding the cave and it is closed to the public.

There are several resort hotels at Shoal Bay. **Shoal Bay Villas** has thirteen spacious one- and two-bedroomed suites and studio units with full kitchens. There is a freshwater pool and restaurant on site. Next door is **Shoal Bay Resort Hotel** with twenty-six ocean-view units with balconies. Maid service and kitchenette are standard. **Fountain Beach** stands at the western end of the bay and is very private and secluded. It has ten studio apartments, its own restaurant and pool and future plans include tennis courts. Close to the beach and all its facilities is **Allamanda**, with sixteen one- and two-bedroomed units.

Head back to the main road and turn left. After about four miles you will reach the fishing village of **Island Harbour,** so named because of the small island in the harbour. Most of the lobsters caught on the island come from this area and at one time they were exported to Puerto Rico, St Martin and some of the other islands. However, greater demand in Anguillian hotels in recent years means that most are now sold locally. Fishermen from Island Harbour go to Scrub Island and further out to Little England and are often willing to take a visitor out on a trip with them. A walk along the beach to see the

Island Harbour – centre for lobster fishing   (MICHAEL BOURNE)

115

RESTAURANTS IN SHOAL BAY
AND ISLAND HARBOUR

Shoal Bay	*Island Harbour*
La Fontana	Cyril's Fish House
Round Rock	Scilly Cay
Madeariman Reef	Hibernia
Uncle Ernie's	Smitty's
Reefside	
Serenity	

A WEDDING IN PARADISE

More and more people are looking for an unusual place to be married.

All you need to be married in Anguilla by a minister or magistrate are:

passport, divorce papers (if any) written in English, twenty-four hours to obtain a licence and a fee of US$284

The perfect place for a wedding – the garden island of Scilly Cay

(EUDOXIE WALLACE)

boats and lobster traps will give you the atmosphere of this northerly Anguillian beach.

The **Arawak Beach Resort** here is set on the site of an ancient Arawak Indian village (see Chapter 10, page 57). It has eighteen villas, its own restaurant, and diving and snorkelling are available. The resort's mini-museum contains, among other things, a small collection of Arawak artefacts: stone tools (axes, grinding stones and scrapers), three-pointed objects or zemis (some carved in zoomorphic form) and pottery sherds. A short boat trip across the harbour brings you to the tiny island of **Scilly Cay** which gives the harbour its name. The island has been transformed by Eudoxie and Sandra Wallace and is a good place to relax and enjoy a good lunch, swim and snorkel. On certain days there is a live band so if you like music it is a good idea to make some enquiries locally and plan your visit accordingly.

Zemi head carved from conch shell   (NICK DOUGLAS AND PENNY SLINGER)

| 21 |
The North-East

More remote and less frequently visited by tourists, the beaches on this stretch of the island are characterised by rugged terrain, rocky shores and pounding seas, providing an exhilarating experience for the more adventurous visitor.

To get there, turn left off the Island Harbour Road about half a mile from the village, on to a road signposted 'Palm Grove Restaurant'. This is a very rough road but soon becomes a sandy track which you follow for about one and a half miles, keeping to the left turns, until you reach **Captain's Bay**. This is an ideal picnic place and good for swimming although it can be rough at times with some undercurrents. Drive for another one and a quarter miles to **Windward Point Bay**, or park and walk part of this road until you reach the coast. The sea here is usually extremely rough and has dangerous currents, so swimming is not recommended, but you can enjoy a walk along the rocky shore northwards, keeping your eyes open for the many different varieties of sponge to be found on the beach.

You will see a pinnacle of grey limestone rocks which appear to have been placed by some giant to provide steps for the casual walker to climb. Amongst the rocks are several types of cacti, especially the melocactus or turk's cap (see Chapter 7, page 35), which are clustered together in groups and look very attractive. The walk is not as difficult as it looks and the strong breeze is very refreshing. From the top you will be rewarded with a view of seas pounding on the rocky coast. Looking north-east you see Scrub Island and the island of Little Scrub. The sea between Scrub Island and the mainland is notoriously choppy and sailors have a difficult task at times through those waters. Looking south there is an extensive area of scrubby, uninhabited land and a view of St Martin to the south-east. You can also see Island Harbour and the north-west coast. It is a perfect place to relax and enjoy the views and is a delight for the photographer. Explore as you will.

The rugged shoreline of Windward Point *opposite*   (ANDRIOLA/CARTY)

Before returning to the main road, follow the sandy road south and you will reach **Savannah Bay**, one of the few bays where body or board surfing is usually possible. It is an extensive bay and it is worth walking the length of it. The offshore reef offers some fascinating snorkelling. At the northern point, which is **Junk's Hole Bay**, there is a small beach restaurant.

The next bay to the south is **Sile Bay**, which unfortunately has been almost entirely spoilt by sand mining in the past. There are now strict rules about sand mining and it is only allowed in a few specified places. Further south again is **Mimi Bay** which is very secluded, with a reef very close to the shore allowing safe swimming in shallow water. There are some good walking areas on the rocks to the south. **East End Pond** is an excellent area for bird watching and most of the pond birds can be seen here (see Chapter 8, page 40).

The **St Augustine Anglican Church** at East End is situated on the site of an abandoned sugar estate. In 1882 Dr Henry Thomas Flemming transferred a small portion of the estate to Bishop William Walrond Jackson for the purpose of building a church and school from the ruins of the Flemmings' mansion which had been destroyed by fire many years earlier. Repair work on the ruins commenced in 1888 and the stone building, with a wooden floor and gabled roof covered with shingles, was completed in 1890. It served the dual purpose of church and school until 1918 when the East End school was opened. A portion of the original building remains intact but the church was completely modernized in the 1980s and is now a combination of traditional and modern. There is a beautiful eastern window patterned with coloured glass which glows brightly at morning service. It was designed in England and financed by St Mary's Church in Slough, where many Anguillians are members.

Sandy Hill Bay is well worth a visit. There is particularly good snorkelling from this bay, both to the east towards Sea Feathers Bay and in the opposite direction to the point. It is interesting to walk towards the cliffs to the south, beyond Long Pond Bay. Good shoes are recommended as the rocks are very sharp. There are several caves, a blow hole and further south there is a natural bridge formed by the rocks across a tiny beach. Long Salt Pond was used at one time for salt production and in the late 1970s experiments in shrimp farming were made here.

On some maps there is a fort marked at Sandy Hill but there is nothing remaining of this today. Little is recorded in the history books about the actual building but it is known that the French were fought and beaten here in 1796 (see Chapter 10, page 59). Sandy Hill was also the scene of some action at the time of the revolution, as it

Sandy Hill Bay (MICHAEL BOURNE)

was here, at the home of Colonel Howard, that William Whitlock, British Parliamentary Under-Secretary of State for Foreign and Commonwealth Affairs, was held for some hours. Eventually shots were fired by the armed mob outside and Whitlock and his party were forced to leave the island. (See Chapter 11 page 67.)

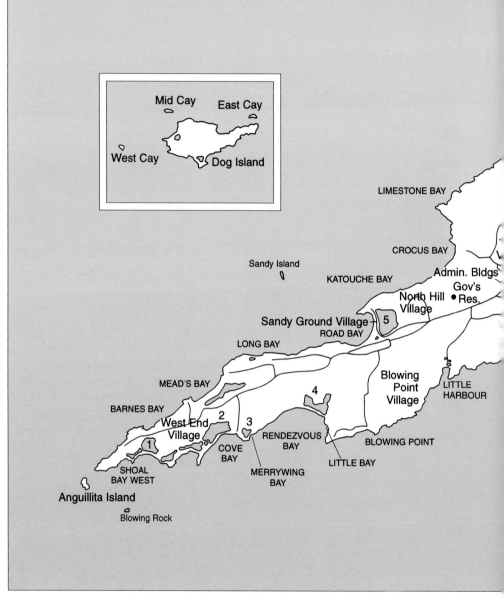

CARIBBEAN

Mid Cay   East Cay

West Cay   Dog Island

LIMESTONE BAY

CROCUS BAY

Sandy Island

KATOUCHE BAY

Admin. Bldgs
Gov's
North Hill   ● Res.
Village

Sandy Ground Village — 5

ROAD BAY

LONG BAY

Blowing
Point
Village   LITTLE
HARBOUR

MEAD'S BAY

4

BARNES BAY

West End   2
Village   3

BLOWING POINT

RENDEZVOUS
BAY

1

COVE
BAY

LITTLE BAY

SHOAL
BAY WEST

MERRYWING
BAY

Anguillita Island

Blowing Rock

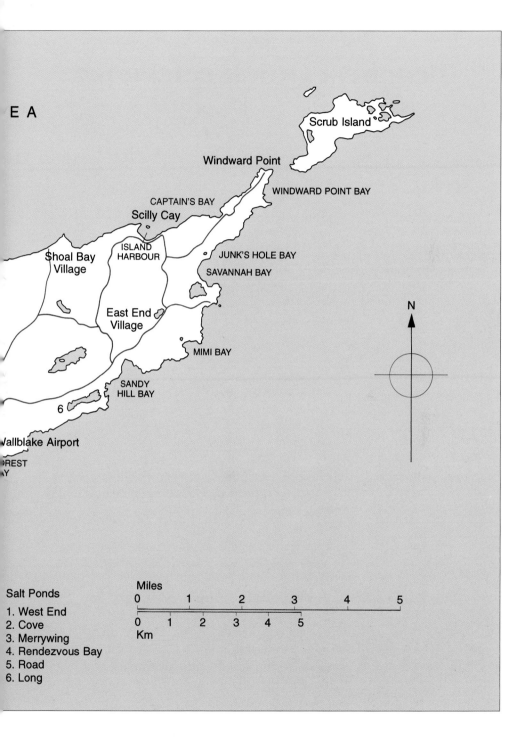

E A

Scrub Island

Windward Point

WINDWARD POINT BAY

CAPTAIN'S BAY

Scilly Cay

ISLAND
HARBOUR

JUNK'S HOLE BAY

Shoal Bay
Village

SAVANNAH BAY

East End
Village

MIMI BAY

N

SANDY
HILL BAY

6

Wallblake Airport

OREST
AY

Salt Ponds

1. West End
2. Cove
3. Merrywing
4. Rendezvous Bay
5. Road
6. Long

Miles

| 0 | 1 | 2 | 3 | 4 | 5 |

Km

| 0 | 1 | 2 | 3 | 4 | 5 |

| 22 |
Beaches: Quick reference

Beach	Features
Barnes Bay	Good swimming and snorkelling. Meta Resort of Anguilla.
Blowing Point	Ferry port for St Martin. Ferries run every half hour. Fishing village to east of jetty. Ferry Boat Inn and apartments to west. West side is good for swimming; interesting spit of sand and reef.
Captain's Bay	Very secluded. Good for picnicking. Can be dangerous for swimming so care is needed.
Cove Bay	One mile of beach and sand dunes, good swimming and walking.
Crocus Bay	Good for swimming and snorkelling. Fishing village so not as private as most beaches. Restaurant and bar.
Forest Bay	Indifferent beach but interesting seaweed beds and reef. Restaurant.
Island Harbour	Fishing village, interesting for boats and lobster traps. Not recommended for swimming. Arawak Beach Resort. Small island in harbour, Scilly Cay, with restaurant and live music, ideal for swimming and snorkelling.
Junk's Hole Bay	At northern end of Savannah Bay. Very calm and shallow, good for young children. Restaurant.

Beach	Features
Katouche Bay	Swimming fair, watch out for currents. Manchineel trees on the beach, poisonous fruit and leaves. Good walk through wooded area behind beach. Small pond with bird life.
Limestone Bay	Small bay, usually good for swimming and snorkelling but can be rough. Secluded.
Little Bay	Access from road a little difficult, climb down the cliff to beach. Easier access from the sea. Good swimming and exceptional snorkelling. Marine park area, nursery for many fish. Bird life around cliffs, especially tropic bird and frigate bird. Secluded.
Little Harbour	Calm, shallow sea, fairly good for swimming. Mangroves at pond behind beach and good bird life. Cinnamon Reef Hotel and restaurant.
Long Bay	Access not easy. Swimming quite good. Good for walking.
Maunday's Bay	Excellent swimming. Very calm. Restaurant. Cap Juluca Hotel.
Mead's Bay	Nearly one mile of beautiful beach, swimming usually good, rough at times. Quiet. Malliouhana Hotel, La Sirena Hotel, Frangipani Beach Club and Carimar Beach Club. Several restaurants.
Merrywing Bay	Good snorkelling. Sonesta Beach Resort and restaurant.
Mimi Bay	Shallow swimming, reef close to shore. Interesting dead coral on beach. Secluded. Pleasant walking on rocks.
Rendezvous Bay	Good swimming, over a mile of beach, walking. Rendezvous Hotel, The Great House (restaurant). Sailing equipment (sunfish, aquafin, sail boats, kayaks) from The Great House, guests have preference.

Windward Point Bay (ANDRIOLA/CARTY)

Beach	Features
Road Bay	Fishing village and commercial port but still very good for swimming and walking. Dive shop. Several restaurants.
Sandy Hill Bay	Excellent snorkelling on both sides of bay. Good for swimming. Good walking on cliffs to south, caves and pond.
Savannah Bay	Best beach for body or board surfing. Good swimming and walking. Offshore reef.
Shoal Bay	One mile of excellent beach. Excellent swimming and snorkelling near shallow or deeper reef. Snorkelling equipment for hire. Also chairs, mats, pedal boats for hire and glass bottomed boat trips. Several restaurants, Shoal Bay Villas and Resort Hotel. Fountain Cavern nearby.
Shoal Bay West	Good swimming and snorkelling. Restaurant. Beach apartments: Cove Castles and Blue Waters. Nearby salt pond with bird life.
Windward Point Bay	Usually very rough and dangerous for swimming. Good area for walking.

| 23 |
Day tours

There are several options for day tours whilst you holiday in Anguilla. The offshore cays or islands are exciting to visit, with unspoilt beaches where you can relax, coral reefs for snorkelling, and birds and other wildlife to see. A day spent visiting one of the neighbouring islands is also worthwhile.

Sandy Island

Sandy Island lies approximately two miles from Sandy Ground and is a perfect small tropical island with a few palm trees and white sand beaches. It is surrounded by coral reef which is alive with reef fish and other marine life. The water depth varies from three feet (1 m) to ten feet (3 m) or more, so snorkelling can be enjoyed by the beginner as well as the more adventurous. It is an ideal way to spend a quiet day or half day.

There are boats which leave the jetty by the marine base at Sandy Ground, every hour from 10 am to 3 pm. Lunch is available on Sandy Island and you can rent snorkelling equipment there.

Scrub Island, Prickly Pear and Dog Island

These other offshore islands are equally attractive for a day's outing, which can be arranged by contacting one of the catamaran or power-boat services. Prickly Pear has a restaurant but the others have none so take a supply of cold drinks with you unless the boat charter is offering this. There are many opportunities for sun bathing, snorkelling, swimming and walking.

St Martin/St Maarten

The unique island of St Martin/St Maarten is the smallest island in the world to be shared by two nations, the northern part of the island belonging to the French and the southern part to the Dutch. Marigot,

ST MARTIN/ST MAARTEN

There is an amusing story about the division of the island of St Martin/St Maarten.

A Dutchman and a Frenchman were supposed to have set off in opposite directions from a point on the coastline. The line between the departure point and the meeting place was to form the border.

Since the French have the larger share of the island, presumably the Frenchman walked the fastest, although other tales suggest the Dutchman stopped for a snooze after too much wine or was delayed by a pretty French girl!

on the French side, can be reached by ferry from Blowing Point and a late ferry back means you can spend some time in St Martin and enjoy some late shopping and dinner there before your return to Anguilla. (See Chapter 24, page 135 for ferry times.) Alternatively you can fly there by WINAIR, Tyden Air or LIAT, a flight of just seven minutes.

St Martin/St Maarten is a beautiful island, not much bigger than Anguilla, with green hills, an indented coastline and some lovely white sandy beaches. The border between the two sides is barely noticeable, but each side reflects the character of the mother nation. It is very pleasant to walk around the town of Marigot visiting sidewalk cafes and wandering through the shops near the marina, savouring the French atmosphere. If you can speak French it will be a bonus. There is a fascinating market near the harbour which sells a variety of craft items and T-shirts.

The Dutch side of the island, St. Maarten, is more developed, with a thriving tourist industry. The main town of Philipsburg is much busier than Marigot, especially if there are any cruise ships in the harbour. It is good for shopping, in particular for duty-free jewellery, cameras, electrical goods, tablecloths and crystal. There are a number of casinos here and both Marigot and Philipsburg have some good art galleries. Philipsburg is easily reached from Marigot by one of the frequent buses or by taxi.

If you wish to see more of the island, it is advisable to rent a car. The island can be seen easily in one day and you can visit many of the beaches and resorts. However, if you mostly want to shop, it is better to use public transport as parking can be difficult.

The St Martin Ferry *opposite* (MICHAEL BOURNE)

St Barthélemy

Fifteen miles south-east of St Martin lies the small island of St Barthélemy, or St Barths, as it is usually called. At one time it belonged to Sweden, hence the name of the capital, Gustavia, after a Swedish king, Gustaf III. However, it is now a French island, its inhabitants descendants of Norman and Breton fishermen and farmers. It is a very pretty island with more vegetation than Anguilla and some good beaches and has been compared to the south of France with its good shopping and attractive sidewalk cafes. Unique to the island are straw hats and other small items, plaited by hand by the women, which make good souvenirs.

There are several boat excursions to St Barths from Anguilla; the *Excellence* or *The Link* take about an hour to motor there whilst the thirty-five foot (11 m) catamaran *Chocolat* at Sandy Ground (see Chapter 17, page 101) takes four hours or more, according to the weather conditions. On certain days early flights by WINAIR or Tyden Air arrive at about 9 am so that you can spend a whole day on the island and return to Anguilla in the evening. The island can be explored easily in one day, allowing time for a tour as well as time to shop.

Other neighbouring islands such as Saba, St Eustatius, Antigua and Montserrat probably require an overnight stay due to flying schedules, but it is always possible to charter a plane for such excursions. (See Chapter 24, page 135.)

| 24 |
What else you need to know

Climate

The climate is tropical with average year-round temperatures of 80–85°F (27–30°C). There is a pleasant breeze nearly all the time and rainfall is low. There are no specific rainy months, although May and November are usually less dry than at other times.

Currency and banking

The official currency is the Eastern Caribbean (EC) dollar, valued at around $2.68 to the US dollar. This is used in all the local groceries and stores, although US dollars are always acceptable.

In restaurants and hotels prices are quoted in US dollars. Most places include a 15% service charge in the bill, but you may still tip if you wish to.

Banks open from 8 am–3 pm Monday to Thursday, and 8 am– 5 pm on Friday.

Customs

Personal effects and baggage compatible with the intended stay are allowed to be brought into Anguilla duty-free. The importation of drugs, firearms and obscene material is prohibited and there are severe penalties for smuggling.

Departure tax

There is a departure tax from the airport and the ferry terminal.

Electricity

110 volts is used throughout the island, as on the US mainland.

**HOLIDAYS IN
ANGUILLA**

New Year's Day
Good Friday
Easter Monday
Labour Day (May)
Anguilla Day (30 May)
Whit Monday
Queen's Birthday (June)
August Monday
August Thursday
Constitution Day (August)
Separation Day (19 December)
Christmas Day
Boxing Day

Passport requirements

Passports are preferred although it is possible to enter Anguilla with a valid driver's licence with photograph if you are a U.S. or Canadian citizen. British citizens must have a passport. A return or onward ticket is also necessary.

Shopping

Shopping in Anguilla is limited: there are a few boutiques in The Valley and in the hotels. Souvenirs are available from the Anguilla Drug Store, the Arts and Crafts Centre and the Devonish Art Gallery, also in The Valley (see Chapter 4, page 16).

There are several groceries which import goods from the USA and the UK and stock most items required by tourists. You may like to bring your own brand of sunblock and insect repellant, although these are available locally.

Visitors are requested to be respectably dressed in shops.

Sports

Water sports are available for guests at most of the hotels. In addition some of the hotels will rent to non-guests. The catamaran *Chocolat* has various cruise offers and is located at Sandy Ground. (See Chapter 17, page 101.) Sandy Island Enterprises has regular hourly trips to Sandy Island for snorkelling and can arrange cruises to many other offshore islands. Scuba diving can be arranged at The Dive Shop at Sandy Ground. (See Chapter 9, page 45.) Tennis is available at hotels, most of which will take bookings from non-guests. Horse riding from El Rancho Del Blues offers trail or beach rides and riding lessons. There are mountain bikes and regular bikes for rent.

Telecommunications

Cable and Wireless provides an excellent telephone, fax and internet service world-wide. Visitors can rent a cellular phone for just US$10 per day and stay in touch with business whilst relaxing.

Radio Anguilla is the Government radio service on AM 1505. ZJF 105.3 is the local FM station. There is cable television with over twenty US channels, two local channels (3 and 9) and a tourist channel (32).

The main post office is in The Valley and is open Monday–Friday, 8 am–3.30 pm.

Phone numbers for all the above are listed in the special tourist section of the telephone book.

Time zone

Anguilla is on Atlantic Standard Time. It is the same as Eastern Standard Time from April–October. In October and on through to April the time in Anguilla is one hour ahead of Eastern Standard Time. Anguilla is four hours behind Greenwich Mean Time.

Tourism Agencies

Anguilla Tourist Board
PO Box 60
The Valley
ANGUILLA
Tel: 809 497 2759

Anguilla also has several official agencies abroad:

Ruth Buckmaster
Windotel
3 Espirus Road
London
SW6 7WJ
UK
Tel: 171 937 7725

Joan Medhurst and Associates
775 Park Avenue
New York 11743
USA
Tel: 800 533 4939

Rita Morozow
c/o Sergat Deutschland
Fieldstrasse 26
D 64319 Pfungstadt
GERMANY
Tel: 49 6157 87816

Barbara Saleh
World Trade Centre
Suite 250
San Francisco
CA 94111
USA
Tel: 415 398 3231

Transportation

Taxis are readily available at the airport and ferry terminal. Rental cars are easily available but in the high season it may be advisable to book ahead of time. Driving permits are required and are obtainable from the car rental agency on production of a valid driver's licence. Drive on the left side of the road. There is a very limited bus service but many taxi operators offer tours of the island at reasonable rates.

Travel: To Anguilla

By air from Puerto Rico: American Eagle flies direct from San Juan to Anguilla, usually by a forty-seater aeroplane with a flying time of approximately one hour. During the high season (December–April) there are four flights daily; at other times of the year just one or two.
By air from St Maarten: Tyden Air flies from St Maarten and connects with many of the airlines arriving there. It is a seven-minute

flight. Tyden is available for charters from St Maarten and can be contacted at the airport there. Advanced booking is possible by phoning toll free from the USA 1 800 842 0261 or directly or 809 497 2719. WINAIR flies from St Maarten to Anguilla and offers several tours to nearby islands.

By air from Antigua: LIAT flies from Antigua and connects with British Airways (BA) flights from London. The airline usually has a special offer for Caribbean travel which includes all the islands.

By ferry from St Martin: There is a regular ferry service between Marigot, St Martin and Blowing Point, Anguilla. Ferries leave St Martin every half hour from 8 am until 7 pm, with an evening ferry leaving at 10.45 pm. Fares are paid on board but departure tax is necessary and make sure your name is on the manifest.

By private yacht: If you arrive by yacht you need to check with immigration and customs at Road Bay or Blowing Point. To sail anywhere else around the island you must have a cruising permit, the price of which depends on the tonnage of the boat. A mooring permit is required to anchor in the Marine Parks: this costs US$15.00 per day. Both permits can be obtained from the marine base at Road Bay, Sandy Ground (see Chapter 9, page 51 and Chapter 17, page 100).

Travel: From Anguilla

By air: American Eagle provides a regular service to Puerto Rico. Tyden Air, LIAT, WINAIR and Air Anguilla operate regular schedules and charter flights to the other Caribbean islands.

By ferry: Ferries leave Blowing Point for St Martin every half hour from 7.30 am until 7 pm with one evening ferry at 10.15 pm. There are several excursions to St Barths, Sandy Island, Scrub Island, Prickly Pear and Dog Island (see Chapter 23, page 127).

Useful telephone numbers

Emergency

Police	911	Hospital	2551
Fire	911	Dental	2343
Ambulance	911		

Airlines

American Eagle	3501	Tyden Air	2719
WINAIR	2748	Air Anguilla	2643
LIAT	5000		

Tourism Department
2759

Courier Service

DHL	3400	Fed Ex	2719
UPS	2239		

Boat Charters

Excellence	4315	Chocolat	3394
The Link	3290	Sandy Island Enterprises	5643

Water

Every building in Anguilla, including homes, apartments and hotels, has its own cistern to collect and store rainfall from the roof and other catchment areas. The cistern is usually built into the house, quite often under the porch or verandah, and in private homes may range in size from 5000 to 50 000 gallons. Often the cistern provides the only water supply and is still the most important source of water for the majority of Anguillians. However, there is a government water supply available as well, and this may be used as an alternative to the cistern water. Some of the larger hotels and the private water suppliers have their own desalination plants. All the water is safe to drink, although visitors are advised to drink bottled water.

opposite (MICHAEL BOURNE)

Sunset over Road Bay (BRENDA CARTY)